Gambling In India: Past, Present and Future

Edited by

Sanju George
Jaisoorya TS

PEEPEE
PUBLISHERS AND DISTRIBUTORS (P) LTD.

Gambling in India: past, present and future

Published by
Pawaninder P. Vij and Anupam Vij
Peepee Publishers and Distributors (P) Ltd.
Head Office: 160, Shakti Vihar, Pitam Pura
Delhi-110 034 (India)

Correspondence Address:
7/31, First Floor, Ansari Road, Daryaganj
New Delhi-110 002 (India)

Ph: 65195868, 23246245, 9811156083

e-mail: peepee160@yahoo.co.in

e-mail: peepee160@rediffmail.com

e-mail: peepee160@gmail.com

www.peepeepub.com

First Edition: 2018

ISBN: 978-81-8445-241-9

Foreword

Gambling is said to be as old as civilization itself. It is well known that various forms of gambling have existed in India for centuries, from the Vedic times onwards.During the past couple of decades, India has been going through a period of rapid sociocultural transformation, urbanization, modernization and globalization of its economy. With the flourishing of India's economy, the middle class population is steadily growing. It is widely recognized that there has been a dramatic increase in alcohol consumption in India in recent years. Most urban areas across the country have witnessed rapid mushrooming of bars and increase in number of liquor stores. Along with the growing alcohol consumption, is love for gambling too increasing in India? Is gambling an addictive behaviour? Does India have a problem with gambling addiction? Are there any adverse consequences due to gambling to a gambler and his/her family? What is the nature, extent and impact of gambling related harmat a population level in India? How can such harm be dealt with? The answers to these questions are not easy to come by.

Most forms of gambling are illegal in most parts of India. Scandals related to sports betting in cricket-mad India are very well known. India's gambling market, just the illegalone alone, is estimated to be worth billions of dollars. With a growing tech savvy young population and rapid expansion of mobile and internet networks and smart phones, newer forms of gambling other than the traditional ones, through internet betting sites, addictive gaming etc. are likely to increase. The gambling laws in India are archaic. There have not been any efforts to review, revise or reform these laws. Should gambling be legalized in India?

There is currently a glaring lacunae of reliable and authentic information on various aspects of the gambling scenario in India. Mental health professionals including psychiatrists are unaware or inadequately informed about gambling related issues. "Gambling in India: Past, Present and Future", a multi-authored book on different aspects of gambling in India,the first of its kind in the country, is a major contribution to fill this void. Edited by two psychiatrists, one of whom is an internationally recognized opinion leader in the field of gambling addictionwho has extensively studied gambling in India, the book provides an excellent overview of the problem of gambling from the Indian perspective. Besides mental health professionals such as psychiatrists and clinical psychologists, the galaxy of 14 contributing authors include a well-known senior journalist from a leading and widely circulated news publication and a practicinglawyer who is a legal academic and writer. Many of the authors are faculty and staff of the Centre for Addiction Medicine at the prestigious National Institute of Mental Health and Neurosciences (NIMHANS), in Bangalore.

"Gambling in India: Past, Present and Future" covers quite comprehensively issues related to causation, identification, assessment and management of gambling disorder and care for families and those affected by gambling, from a clinical as well as a public health perspective. The need for legislative reforms of gambling laws, and the need for further research on gambling in India are highlighted. The authors speculate that gambling and gambling related harm are likely to increase in India over the years and offer several suggestions and recommendations to deal with them and guide public policy..

The book will be of immense value to practitioners, researchers and students of various aspects of mental health care from different disciplinary backgrounds such as medicine (psychiatry), nursing, psychology and social work. It should find a place in the library of every centre where mental health professionals and workers are trained. Policy makers and legislators interested in the area of public health, addiction and gambling will find the book quite useful. It is hoped that this authoritative publication will pave the way for serious discussion and debate on the vicissitudes of gambling in India and contribute to public policy development and legislative reforms.

Mohan Isaac

Clinical Professor of Psychiatry,
The University of Western Australia, Perth,
Australia & Visiting Professor of Psychiatry,
NIMHANS, Bangalore, India

Preface

Gambling as a pastime has always been popular in India and continues to be so even in present-day India. Currently, most forms of gambling are illegal in India except for the state-run lotteries (and that too only in some states), horse racing, rummy card games and casinos (in only two of the twenty nine states). However many Indians gamble illegally: India has a huge illegal betting market and betting on sports such as cricket is extremely popular.

Despite this, gambling in India is seldom seen as a potentially addictive behaviour in academic discourse, policy debate or clinical patient-doctor assessments, and consequently has received little attention from academics, policy makers and mental health professionals. However some of this is beginning to change: research has emerged recently suggesting that gambling and gambling-related problems are a matter of concern among Indians. Also, the Indian Psychiatric Society (file:///C:/Users/sanju.george/Downloads/OTHER%20PUTATIVE%20BEHAVIOURAL%20ADDICTIONS.pdf) in 2015 published a booklet on behavioural addictions and gambling addiction features significantly in it.

To our knowledge there is no single monograph that comprehensively presents an overview of gambling in India - its evolution, its legal aspects, current scale and forms, the illegal gambling scene, research evidence, treatment aspects and challenges for the future. As gambling and gambling addiction are in recent times entering the public's interest and psychiatrists' attention, we see this as an opportune time to bring out this book.

In this book we have brought together a group of eminent scholars from relevant fields, who have the expertise and specialism to discuss their topics with authority and vision. We hope this book will be of interest to mental health professionals and others working in fields where gamblers or their loved ones seek help, academics, researchers and policy makers. Although the discussion here is limited to gambling in India, this book might also interest those outside India, especially those in the developing world where there is dearth of such work. It is our wish and aspiration that this effort of ours will spur further debate and interest in this topic.

Sanju George & Jaisoorya TS

Contributors

Dr. Arun Enara (MBBS, DPM, DNB) trained in psychiatry from the Pushpagiri Institute of Medical Science and Research Centre, Kerala. He is currently pursuing his Diplomate of National Board (DNB) from Bangalore. His areas of interest include stigma, person centered medicine, and portrayal of mental illness in art and movies. He has won several awards including the best outgoing resident and the "Young psychiatrist track award" of the World Congress of Social Psychiatry, 2016 and the "International young psychiatrist travel fellowship" of the World Congress of Psychiatry, 2017.

Dr. Abhijit Nadkarni (MBBS, DPM, MRCPsych, MSc, PhD) is an addiction psychiatrist conducting research aimed at developing and evaluating interventions for alcohol use disorders in low resource settings. He was a Wellcome Trust Clinical Research Fellow at the London School of Hygiene & Tropical Medicine, UK and is currently based in Sangath, Goa where he leads the Addictions Research Group. His research interests encompass global mental health, particularly the epidemiology of addictions in low and middle income countries.

Dr. Arun Kandasamy (MBBS, DPM, MD) is an addiction psychiatrist. He works as an associate professor at the Centre for Addiction Medicine at the National Institute of Mental Health and Neuro Sciences (NIMHANS), Bangalore, India. His areas of interest are addictions in young people, dual diagnosis, behavioural addictions and public health aspects of addiction and related disorders.

George Johnson (MA, LLM) is a lawyer practising at the High Court of Kerala. He is the Editor of Kerala High Court Cases, Kerala Law Decision & Kerala and Central Laws. He has edited more than 30 law books including Laws of Land in Kerala, Law of Land Reforms in Kerala, Law of Motor and Motor Accident Claims in Kerala, Civil Rules of Practice and Criminal Rules of Practice.

Professor YC Janardhanan Reddy (MBBS, DPM, MD) is a Professor of psychiatry at the National Institute of Mental Health and Neuro Sciences (NIMHANS), Bangalore, India. He has been on the faculty of the department of psychiatry at NIMHANS since 1995. He heads the OCD clinic, which is involved in clinical services, post-graduate training and research. His areas of specialization include obsessive compulsive and related disorders, bipolar disorders and clinical psychopharmacology. Prof Reddy has a special interest in studying the long-term course and outcome of OCD, bipolar disorders and the management of treatment resistant OCD. He is also involved in studies of phenomenology, comorbidity, family-genetics, treatment resistance, neuropsychology and neuroimaging of OCD.

Dr. Jayant Mahadevan (MBBS, MD, PDF) is currently pursuing DM in addiction psychiatry at the Centre for Addiction Medicine, NIMHANS, Bangalore. His areas of interest are neurobiology of substance use disorders and vulnerability to addiction, dual diagnosis, training and capacity building, and recent advances in addiction treatment.

Dr. Lokesh Shekhawat (MBBS, MD) started his career as Assistant Professor at the All India Institute of Medical Sciences, Patna, Bihar and initiated psychiatric services there. He is currently working as associate professor in the department of psychiatry at Ram Manohar Lohia Hospital, New Delhi. He runs an OCD clinic and has special interests in obsessive compulsive and related disorders, impulse dyscontrol disorders and sexual disorders. His research interests are closely linked to his clinical interests.

Neeraj Chauhan (senior journalist – investigations, Times of India) works as an assistant editor with The Times of India and specialises in internal security, law enforcement and politics. With over 12 years of experience in print journalism, he has extensively written on counter-terrorism and security issues. As a 2015 Chevening Scholar, Chauhan researched counter-terrorism strategies and their implementation in the United Kingdom.

Professor Richard Velleman (BSc, MSc, PhD, FBPsS, FRSS, C Psychol) is a leading authority on substance misuse, and especially the impact of this misuse on other family members, including children. He is both a clinical and an academic psychologist, has always held simultaneous posts in Universities and in the National Health Service, England), has worked in the addictions and mental health fields for over 40 years, and has published over 200 items including fifteen books, and more than 160 scientific journal papers and book chapters. He is a co-founder and one of the Trustees of AFINet <http://www.afinetwork.info/>, the International Network, concerned with Addiction and the Family; and is Senior Research Fellow with the Sangath Community Health NGO, Goa, India <http://www.sangath.com/> and Co-Director of the Addictions Research Group, where he is developing and researching novel ways to deliver psychological interventions to people with serious addiction or mental health problems. He was for 6 years (2008-2013) a member of the 15-person Scientific Committee of the EMCDDA (European Monitoring Centre on Drugs and Drug Addiction). He is now Emeritus Professor of Mental Health Research at the University of Bath, England.

Dr. Roy Abraham Kallivayalil (MBBS, DPM, MD) is Vice- Principal and professor & head, department of psychiatry, Pushpagiri Institute of Medical Sciences, Thiruvalla, Kerala, India. He is the Secretary General of the World Psychiatric Association (2014-2020) and President of World Association for Social Psychiatry (2016-19). He is also the National Vice-President of Indian Medical Association (2016-17) and President of 'National Alliance for Mental Health'. He was the Secretary General of the World Association for Social Psychiatry (2010-13), President of the Indian Association for Social Psychiatry (2007-08 and 2010-11), General Secretary (2002-06) and President of Indian Psychiatric Society (2012-13), founder Secretary General of the SAARC Psychiatric Federation and Associate Editor, Indian Journal of Psychiatry (2007-11). He is a member of the editorial board of World Psychiatry and the International Journal of Person-Centred Medicine, international advisor of the Japanese society of psychiatry and neurology (2017-19) and international distinguished fellow of American Psychiatric Association since 2013.

Dr. Sanju George (MBBS, FRCPsych) is a senior consultant psychiatrist at Rajagiri hospital in Kochi, India. Immediately prior to this he worked as an addiction psychiatrist in the UK for fifteen years. As an academic he has authored over 120 papers in international journals. An opinion leader in the field of gambling addiction, he researches, writes and speaks on the subject, and collaborates nationally and internationally. Some of his work in this field include: over 30 published papers, authored the Royal College of Psychiatrists' policy paper on gambling addiction, co-edited UK's first textbook on problem gambling, and served on the UK government's Responsible Gambling Strategy Board, the body that advises the government on gambling - related issues. He is the only researcher to have extensively studied gambling in India.

Dr. Srinivas Balachander (MBBS, MD, PDF) is currently a senior resident in the department of Psychiatry at NIMHANS, Bangalore. He completed his MD in psychiatry from Post Graduate Institute of Medical Education & Research, Chandigarh and did a post-doctoral fellowship in Obsessive-Compulsive & Related Disorders at NIMHANS. His academic & research interests include the neurobiology, pharmacotherapy and intensive residential treatment for OCD, body dysmorphic disorder, trichotillomania & Tourette's syndrome.

Dr. Jaisoorya TS (MBBS, DCP, MD, MRCPsych) is an associate professor of psychiatry at NIMHANS, Bangalore, India. He completed his MD (Psychiatry) from the NIMHANS and has been on the faculty of the department of psychiatry at NIMHANS since 2015. His areas of specialization include obsessive-compulsive and related disorders, and public mental health. His research projects and publications are also in these areas. During his clinical and academic career he has received several awards: the Daniel Cappon Prize *proxime accessit*' awarded by the Imperial College, London(2005);Royal Society of Medicine, UK – Section of Psychiatry – Mental Health Foundation Essay Prize in 2006; and the Kerala Catholic Bishop Council Award for meritorious de-addiction services in 2014.

Professor Vivek Benegal (MBBS, DPM, MD) is professor of psychiatry and head, Centre for Addiction Medicine, Department of Psychiatry, NIMHANS, India. His areas of research interest include epidemiology of alcohol misuse in India; research on substance use and its impact on under-researched, high-risk, hidden populations; neurobiology and genetics of alcohol dependence; translational research; and policy and advocacy. He has over 500 academic publications and is a member of advisory and drafting committees of national legislation pertaining to the Narcotic Drugs and Psychotropic Substances Act and national alcohol policy, as well as the alcohol policies of various state governments. Some of his recent/ ongoing funded research include: Consortium on Vulnerability to Externalizing Disorders and Addiction (c VEDA), funded by Medical Research Council, UK & Indian Council of Medical Research, India; Accelerator Programme for Stem Cells in Human Disease, funded by Department of Biotechnology, India; and National Mental Health Survey of India, funded by the Ministry of Health, Government of India.

Contents

Chapter 1

History and evolution of gambling in India

Vivek Benegal and Sanju George

History of gambling in India

Gambling prevailed as a popular pastime in ancient India as evidenced from its depiction in several ancient texts and epics written in Tamil and Sanskrit before the Common Era (BCE) (Benegal, 2013).

In this chapter, we will look at two such portrayals of gambling addiction from ancient India, one in the Rig Veda and one in the Mahabharata. Then we will trace its presence and influence in Indian society during the medieval and colonial periods, including the origins of the Public Gaming Act of 1867. Gambling and gambling addiction post-independence (1947 onwards), as it existed and continues to do so are also briefly described.

Gambling in ancient India

One of the earliest accounts of gambling anywhere in the world is in a hymn from the Rig Veda, an ancient Indian text written between 1700 and 1100 BCE. There are few clearer descriptive accounts of gambling's phenomenology, psychopathology and adverse consequences (Bhide, 2007). Part of this hymn (from the tenth book of the Rig Veda (Singh, 1990) is given below, where a gambler addresses the dice which has destroyed his life and begs to spare him:

The Gambler:

These nuts that once tossed on tall trees in the wind
but now smartly roll over the board, how I love them!
As alluring as a draught of Soma on the mountain,
the lively dice have captured my heart.

My faithful wife never quarrelled with me
or got angry; to me and my companions

she was always kind, yet I've driven her away
for the sake of the ill-fated throw of a die.

Chorus:

His wife's mother loathes him, his wife rejects him,
he implores people's aid but nowhere finds pity.
A luckless gambler is no more good
than an aged hack to be sold on the market.

Other men make free with the wife of a man
whose money and goods the eager dice have stolen.
His father and mother and brothers all say,
"He is nothing to us. Bind him, put him in jail!"

The Gambler:

I make a resolve that I will not go gaming.
So my friends depart and leave me behind.
But as soon as the brown nuts are rattled and thrown,
to meet them I run, like an amorous girl.

Chorus:

To the meeting place the gambler hastens.
Shall I win? He asks himself, hoping and trembling,
but the throws of the dice ruin his hopes,
giving the highest scores to his opponent.

Dice, believe me, are barbed: they prick and they trip,
they hurt and torment and cause grievous harm.
To the gambler they are like children's gifts, sweet as honey, but
they turn on the winner in rage and destroy him.

Fifty-three strong, this band jumps playfully,
like Savitri, the god whose statutes are true.
They pay no heed to the anger of the powerful;
the king himself bows down before them.
Downward they roll, then jump in the air!
Though handless, they master those who have hands!
Unearthly coals thrown down on the board,
though cold they burn the player's heart to ashes.
Abandoned, the wife of the gambler grieves.

Grieved too, is his mother as he wanders to nowhere.
Afraid and in debt, ever greedy for money,
he steals in the night to the home of another.

He is seized by remorse when he sees his wife's lot,
beside that of another with well-ordered home.
In the morning, however, he yokes the brown steeds
and at the evening falls stupid before the cold embers.

The Gambler to the dice:

To the mighty chieftain of your whole band,
the one who has become the king of your troop,
to him I show my ten fingers extended.
No wealth do I withhold! I speak truly!

Chorus:

Steer clear of dice. Till well your own field.
Rejoice in your portion and value it highly.
See there, O Gambler, your cattle, your wife.
This is the counsel of the noble Savitri.

The Gambler to the dice:

Grant us your friendship, have mercy upon us!
Do not overwhelm us with your fierce attack!
May your anger and evil intention be assuaged!
Let the brown dice proceed to ensnare another!

Depiction of gambling in the Mahabharata

Yudhishthira, the eldest of the five Paandava brothers, is described to have a fatal flaw – he is addicted to gambling (Ganguli & Rajagopalachari 1996).

In the second section of the Mahabharata, the Sabha Parva, Duryodhana, the eldest of the Kauravas (Pandavas' cousins) wants to take revenge on Yudhishthira. So, along with his uncle Shakuni he hatches a plan to exploit Yudhishthira's love for the dice, and invites the Pandavas to the Kaurava capital of Hastinapura.

Although initially Yudhishthira stopped himself from playing, he was taunted by Shakuni and the Kauravas and he gave in. Shakuni played on behalf of his nephew, Duryodhana. As the game progressed Yudhishthira lost his possessions one by one. Chasing his losses, Yudhishthira gambled away his four younger brothers, himself and his wife Draupadi. Although, all his possessions were returned by Duryodhana's father, Dhritarashtra, Yudhishthira played and lost to Shakuni again. It is then that the Paandavas and Draupadi as per the bet had to go into exile for twelve years.

Yudhishthira, despite his numerous virtues is clearly depicted as being addicted to gambling. Despite being fully aware of its perils, he can't stop himself from betting away all that are precious to him.

Apart from the above two, other references to gambling from ancient India prove that gambling was pervasive in India during that period. These include Kathasaritasagar, a collection of legends and folktales, written in the 11th century Common Era (CE) (Somadeva, 1997); The Clay Cart, a classical Sanskrit theatre (Coulson, 1981); and sculptures from that era. It was not only dice games that were popular but also betting on chariot races, cock and ram fights, and other sport.

Gambling in medieval India

Gambling's popularity persisted during the medieval period (8th to 18th century CE) despite much of India being ruled by Islamic dynasties; gambling and drinking were proscribed under Sharia law. Gambling was referred to as maisir, meaning 'monetary gains from chance or speculation'. It is noted that gambling was very popular in the Mughal court. Babur (the founder of the Mughal Empire in India) is 'credited' with introducing a betting game called ganjifa, which many see as a precursor to poker. Having recognised the potential perils of gambling during this period, Aurangzeb, the sixth Mughal, appointed muhtasaibs or censors of public morals to stop people gambling (Mukhia, 1969).

Gambling in colonial India

During Britain's rule of India (from the 17th century to 1947), passion for gambling among the Indian public persisted. Seventeenth century accounts contain references to the 'itch of gambling spreading like a plague' among traders of the East India Company in Surat (Chatterton, 1924). Later in the 18th century, company men are portrayed as 'would-be nabobs who spend much of their time gambling away their fortunes' (Reynolds et al, 2008).

A particular form of numbers gambling called Satta was very popular during the 18th century. In Satta, people would bet on the prices of opium, gold and cotton, or on the amount of rainfall (Hardgrove, 2002).

Despite being aware of the ill-effects of gambling in India, the British actually encouraged some forms of gambling as they stood to gain huge tax revenues from the different forms of gambling. However, as the mood in Britain turned against gambling and its negative impact on society such as bankruptcy, delinquency, crime, etc. anti-gambling legislation began to take shape in British - ruled India too.

It was to restrict and regulate gambling practices in India that the Imperial Legislative Council enacted The Pubic Gambling Act of India in 1867.

The Public Gambling Act 1867

This law, the Public Gambling Act of 1867, remains the only law that regulates gambling in India. It was passed in 1867 with a view to regulate and discourage gambling on games of chance. It restricted most forms of gambling and also discriminated games of pure chance such as Satta (which it made illegal) from games of skill and not just mere chance such as horse racing (which it made legal). Its aim was to provide for the punishment of public gambling and the keeping of common gaming houses in certain parts of British-ruled India (the United Provinces, East Punjab, Delhi and the Central Provinces). More of this is discussed in chapter 3.

In the section below we will provide an overview of the current gambling scene in India (gambling legislation, types of gambling, etc.), will briefly discuss casino-based gambling in Goa, and also describe in some detail what is known about gambling in Kerala, a South Western state of India, with a population of 30 million people. Kerala was selected as an illustrative example as it was possible to obtain gambling-related data from the state government.

Extent of gambling in present-day India

The only legal forms of gambling in India are state-run lotteries (only in some states), horse racing (six states), rummy card games and casinos (in two states). Lotteries are legal in only 12 states and 5 Union territories but banned in 17 states. Gambling at festival fairs is also very popular in India, as they offer a range of legal and illegal gambling opportunities, collectively referred to as 'festival gambling' (Benegal, 2013).

India also has a huge illegal betting market and betting on cricket is very popular. Although figures are unverifiable, as it is illegal, it was claimed that nearly Rs. 2500 crore [nearly $375 million] was bet on an India vs. West Indies cricket match in 2016 and that Rs. 30,000 crore [nearly $4.4 billion] was bet on the 2016 T 20 Cricket World Cup (The Economic Times, 2016). More information on illegal gambling in India is provided in chapter 4.

Gambling in Goa

Goa is the smallest Indian state by area and has a population of only 1.45 million. It is located along India's South Western coastline.

Goa is only one of two (Sikkim being the other state) Indian states where casinos are legal. Goa also has state-run lotteries. The Directorate of Small Savings and Lotteries (http://goastatelotteries.gov.in/) is the government department responsible for organizing, conducting and promoting lotteries in Goa. It was set up in 2006. The directorate's website states that it uses income from lotteries to help run various social welfare schemes for the poor and under-privileged, old age homes, asylums and a special school.

It is estimated that there are approximately 15 casinos in Goa, of which ten are land-based and the other five are offshore/floating casinos. Goa's casinos had about 15,000 visitors per day in 2014. In total, casinos in Goa have nearly 350 live and electronic table games, and 160 slot machines. Goa generates about 95% of India's total casino- generated income.

Legislation in Goa (The Goa, Daman and Diu Public Gambling Act, 1976) (http://www.daman.nic.in/acts-rules%5CPolicedepartment%5Cdocuments/Public%20Gambling%20Act.pdf) only allows casinos to be set up in five star hotels or offshore, that too only with prior approval from the government. Apparently the Goan government received Rs. 135 crores [$20 million] as revenue from its casinos in 2013 (The Economic Times, 2013). In April 2016, it was made illegal for Goans to enter casinos in Goa. Those in favour of this proposal argue that such a move will protect local people from gambling-related harm. Critics say such legislation condones casino gambling, and that strict implementation will be difficult.

A report published by Global Market Advisors titled 'Gaming in India: An Evaluation of the Market's Potential' in 2016 (http://globalmarketadvisors.com/wp-content/uploads/2016/04/GMA_Gaming-In-India-White-Paper_April28.pdf) states that Indians who gamble in casinos overwhelmingly prefer table games and also card games like roulette, blackjack, baccarat, and poker, and other traditional Indian card games such as Teen Patti, Mini-Flush, Paplu (Rummy), and Andar Bahar.

Gambling landscape of Kerala

Currently, the only legal forms of gambling in Kerala are state-run lotteries and rummy card games. Keralites also engage in various illegal gambling activities at festival fairs, and bet on cricket, although the scale of this is unknown.

The Kerala state-run lottery (the most easily available and the most commonly engaged in gambling activity in the state) was set up in 1967. Kerala state runs seven weekly lotteries and six bumper draws. On an average, between 4 and 4.5 crore tickets are sold each week (4, 05, 13,630 lottery tickets were sold in the7 - day period from 8/8/16 to 14/8/16). 34,417 authorized lottery agents and about a lakh retailers are estimated to work in this field. Of this only 33,249 retailers are registered with the State's Welfare Fund Board (others do it as part - time work). The state government earmarks about 1% of the revenue for the welfare of lottery sellers.

Lotteries Regulation Act 1998 is the Central Act which governs all lottery operations, and the State's finance minister is the chairman of State Level Monitoring Committee of the Karunya scheme.

Table 1.1

Revenue generated from Kerala state - run lotteries

Year	Revenue collection (Rs. crores)	Profit (Rs. crores)	Remarks
2011-12	1287.22	394.87	Approximate net profit is 21% of the total revenue collection. In addition, 3% of revenue collected is paid as sales tax.
2012-13	2778.81	681.77	
2013-14	3793.85	788.43	
2014-15	5445.85	1168.26	
2015-16	6318.47	1461.16	
2016-17 (Up to 17 August)	2902.78	-	

The state government, in 2011, started a new lottery called the "Karunya (meaning kindness) lottery". This state-run lottery gives most of its proceeds to the care of the sick and seriously ill. Please see tables below:

Table 1.2: Revenue and profit generated from Karunya lotteries from 2011-1 onwards is given below:

No	Year	**Collection** from Karunya lotteries **(Rs. crores)**		**Profit from Karunya lotteries (Rs. crores)**	
		Karunya	Karunya plus	Karunya	Karunya plus
1	2011-12	188.87	-	38.96	
2	2012-13	464.61	-	105.25	
3	2013-14	602.10	-	132.02	
4	2014-15	695.27	681.92	141.80	131.40
5	2015-16	803.45	823.91	155.59	147.96
6	2016-17 (13 August)	275.86	261.12	76.66	67.06
TOTAL		**3030.16**	**1766.95**	**650.28**	**346.42**
Grand Total		**4797.11**		**996.70**	

Of the total revenue (profit) generated from Karunya Lotteries, fund allocation as detailed below has been made to Karunya Benevolent Fund Scheme.

Table: 1.3

No	**Year**	**Fund allotted to KBF(Rs. crores)**
1	2011-12	15
2	2012-13	100
3	2013-14	210
4	2014-15	200
5	2015-16	250
6	2016-17	-
	TOTAL	**775**

Karunya lottery: ethical issues

At first glance, Karunya lottery is merely a charitable act with no conceivable harmful effects. And those who hold this view would point to the Rs. 1200 crore rupees it spent on charity over the past five years. Supporters also highlight the several hundred people (and their families) this business employs/ supports financially- as authorized agents, retailers, and other 'unofficial' lottery sellers.

However, critics highlight several concerns many of which are applicable to other state-run lotteries as well:

1. Buying a Karunya lottery ticket is very much an act of gambling and not a mere charitable act as the buyer hopes to win a prize although there might also be charitable reasons for buying the ticket
2. Playing Karunya lottery is perceived to be more socially acceptable (among peers and parents). So it could be argued that more children, women and other vulnerable groups are more likely to start playing the lottery who otherwise may not have done so.
3. There could also be a degree of 'modelling' - i.e. children and young people model their parents' behaviour, in this case buying the lottery.
4. 'Soft' gambling acts such as the Karunya lottery might act as a gateway to other gambling activities/addiction such as betting online, sports betting, etc.
5. Those buying such lottery tickets are not aware of the potential risk for harm- i.e. it becoming a problem or even worse an addiction.

Given these concerns, we call for further debate, especially regarding the ethics of Karunya lottery: Put simply, the question is – does the end justify the means?

Also note that, figures are only available for Kerala state-run lotteries; there are several other lotteries, a range of private betting activities, online gambling and various illegal gambling activities.

Conclusion

In summary, one thing is clear: not only do people in India gamble, some gamble problematically. There is very little awareness among the general public or healthcare professionals about gambling's addictive potential and gambling-related harms: and this needs to be addressed.

Acknowledgement: My sincere gratitude to Dr K M Abraham, IAS, Additional Chief Secretary (Finance), Kerala for providing me information given in the tables in this paper.

Key points

- Gambling has prevailed as a popular pastime in ancient, medieval and colonial India, and it remains so in modern India.
- The Public Gambling Act was introduced in India in 1867 to regulate and discourage gambling on games of chance.
- Currently the only legal forms of gambling in India are state-run lotteries (only in some states), horse racing (six states), rummy card games and casinos (only in Goa and Sikkim).
- India has a huge illegal betting market.

References

Benegal, V. (2013). Gambling experiences, problems and policy in India: a historical analysis. *Addiction*, 108: 2062–2067.
Bhide, A. (2007). Compulsive gambling in ancient Indian texts. *Indian Journal of Psychiatry*, 49 (4): 294–295.
Chatterton, E. (1924). History of the Church of England in India since the Early Days of the East India Company. London: SPCK, Available at: http://anglicanhistory.org/india/chatterton1924/01.html
Coulson, M. (1981). Three Sanskrit Plays. New York: Penguin Classics.
Ganguli, K. M. (1896). Translation of Vyasa's Mahabharata. Available from: http://www.mahabharataonline.com/translation/index.php.
George, S., Kallivayalil, R., Jaisoorya, T. S. (2014). Gambling addiction in India: Should psychiatrists care? Indian Journal of Psychiatry, 56 (2): 111-112.
George, S., Jaisoorya, T.S., Sivasankaran, N.B., Rani, A., Menon, P., Madhavan, R. et al. (2016). A cross-sectional study of problem gambling and its correlates among college students in South India. British Journal of Psychiatry Open, 2 (3):199- 203.
Jaisoorya, T. S., Beena, K. V., Beena, M., Ellangovan, K., Thennarassu, K., Bowden-Jones, H. (2017). Do High School Students in India Gamble? A Study of Problem Gambling and Its Correlates. Journal of Gambling Studies, 33(2):449-460.
Hardgrove, A. (2002). Community as public culture in modern India: The Marwaris in Calcutta 1897-1997. New York: Columbia University Press. Available at: http://www.gutenberg-e.org/haaol/frames/fhaao5.html
Mukhia, H. (1969). Medieval Indian history and the communal approach. In: Thapar R, Mukhia H, Chandra B, editors Communalism and the Writing of Indian history. New Delhi, India; Penguin Books.
Rajagopalachari, C. (1996). The Mahabharata. Bharatiya Vidya Bhavan: Mumbai.
Singh, N. S. (1990). HH Wilson's translation of the Rig Veda Samhita (Enlarged). 2nd ed. Nag Publishers: Delhi.
Somadeva. (1997). Tales from Kathasaritasagara. New Delhi, India. Penguin Classics.
Economic Times, 2016. Wallets Grew Lighter as Hope Stayed Alive Till the Very End. Economic Times, Kochi (2 April)
Economic Times, 2013. Goa Casinos Contribute Rs.135 Crore Revenue in\ 2012 – 13, (13 April).

Chapter 2

Etiology and conceptual models of gambling disorder

Srinivas Balachander and YC Janardhan Reddy

Introduction

The act of gambling is risking something of value in the hope of obtaining something of greater value. Though previously considered as illegal, immoral or disreputable, gambling is now recognized as a legitimate form of leisure and recreation. Persistent and recurrent maladaptive patterns of gambling behaviour that disrupts personal, family, and/or vocational pursuits has now been termed "Gambling Disorder" in the diagnostic and statistical manual of mental disorders (DSM – 5) of the American Psychiatric Association. (APA, 2013)

The last decade has seen a tremendous increase in the number of venues and accessibility for gambling, and most individuals (up to 80% of the American population) have been known to indulge in gambling activities at some point in their lives. However, only very few of them (1%) have problematic patterns of gambling (Petry et al, 2005). On the other hand, studies from India have shown a different pattern, wherein the mere exposure to gambling is more likely to lead to problematic patterns of gambling, with 38% of those who are exposed were found to have gambling disorder (George et al, 2016). With easy access to gambling via the internet, one may logically anticipate an increase in the prevalence of gambling disorders in the near future, especially in India.

Terminological and nosological status

Research on gambling disorder has been confounded by the differing and varying terminologies used. Pathological gambling was probably the first term used to refer to excessive gambling as a mental disorder, introduced by the International Classification of Diseases (ICD-9) and DSM-III, under the category of Impulse Control Disorders Not Elsewhere Classified. The word *"pathological"* is now considered outdated and pejorative, and hence was dropped from DSM - 5. The term **"Gambling disorder"** is now used by the DSM - 5, and it is included in the section of addiction disorders. The position of this disorder is still being debated, and the ICD-11 Working Group for Obsessive Compulsive - Related Disorders (OCRD) has proposed a separate chapter for impulse control disorders that includes pathological gambling, kleptomania, pyromania, compulsive sexual disorder, problematic internet use and intermittent explosive disorder (Grant et al, 2014).

The term *"problem gambling"* has been used interchangeably with pathological gambling in some of the earlier literature on gambling. However, it is now specifically used to refer to a sub-threshold condition, and hence could lead to confusion regarding the severity of the disorder. This distinction between these terms is clear in the two most commonly used gambling screening instruments, the South Oaks Gambling Screen (SOGS) and the National Opinion DSM Screen for Gambling Problems (NODS). Other terms such as compulsive gambling and harmful gambling have been used by certain researchers from time to time but have not been validated.

Etiological factors

Gambling disorder is understood to be a complex, heterogeneous disorder, the etiology of which involves multiple factors interacting with each other. These can largely be divided into neurobiological, psychological and socio-cultural factors. It should be noted that the majority of research over the past two decades has looked at the disorder from the point of it being an addiction disorder. As a result of this, most evidence points to certain alterations in the functioning of the reward system in the brain.

As in the case of substance use disorders, exposure to the object of addiction is a pre-requisite for development of the disorder, and so certain "gambling-related" factors, and socio-cultural factors which may determine the risk of exposure to gambling venues are also discussed. The multitude of factors associated, along with the heterogeneity of its presentation in different individuals may suggest that there may be different subtypes of the disorder.

Neurobiological factors

Gambling disorder can be conceptualized from a neurobiological perspective, in terms of a dysfunctional reward system, with diminished top-down control from pre-frontal cortical regions, coupled with excessive drive from sub cortical regions involved in reward processing. However, controversy still exists as to whether gambling disorder means a hypo-functioning or hyper-functioning reward system. There is a large body of evidence from neurotransmitter-related, neuroimaging and genetic studies.

Neurotransmitters

Emergence of gambling behaviours along with other impulse control disorders in patients with Parkinson's disease after initiation of treatment with dopaminergic agonists, provided some evidence for role of dopamine in the etiology of gambling. Early studies also showed altered levels of monoamine metabolites (5-HIAA, HVA and MHPG) in the CSF of patients with gambling disorders (Bergh et al, 1997, Nordin et al, 1999). Noradrenergic, serotonergic, dopaminergic and opioidergic neurotransmitter systems have been proposed to contribute to arousal/excitement, impulse control, reward/reinforcement, and urges/cravings respectively and their roles have been studied in gambling disorder. To a smaller extent, the roles of glutamate and GABA-ergic systems have also been looked at. The two most important contemporary approaches to study these neurotransmitter systems have been (i) positron emission tomography (PET) using receptor or reuptake channel binding radio-ligands and (ii) genetic studies. Roles of the individual neurotransmitters and the evidence available are discussed below.

Dopamine

Dopamine in the mesolimbic system plays a key role in the modulation of seeking rewards and reinforcements, and hence has been the most extensively studied neurotransmitter in the pathophysiology of gambling (Potenza M, 2013). Dopamine is implicated in attentional processes, learning, motivation and the salience of stimuli, especially rewards. Several reports of newly emergent gambling disorder in patients treated with dopamine receptor agonists for Parkinson's disease, restless legs syndrome and hyperprolactinemia have been published over the years (Pirritano et al, 2014).

Cerebrospinal fluid (CSF) studies have shown low levels of dopamine and high levels of dopamine metabolites, thereby suggesting a high turnover of dopamine in gambling disorder (Bergh et al, 1997). Several allelic variants of the D2 and D4 receptors and the Catechol-O-Methyl Transferase (COMT) gene have been found to occur in increased rates in persons with gambling disorders. Differences in striatal uptake patterns of the dopamine radio ligand C-11 raclopride have been noted in subjects with Parkinson's disease who developed gambling with dopamine agonists versus those who did not develop gambling (Steeves et al, 2009). One raclopride Positron Emission Tomography (PET) study found an "inverted U" relationship between striatal dopamine release and gambling task performance in pathological gamblers but not in controls, suggesting enhanced dopamine sensitivity to uncertainty in gamblers (Linnet, 2012).

Despite all this evidence for the role of dopamine, the use of dopaminergic antagonists (olanzapine, haloperidol, etc.) have not yielded fruitful results in the treatment of gambling disorder (Potenza, 2013). However, pre-clinical trials evaluating antagonists of D4 receptors have yielded promising results (Cocker et al, 2016).

Serotonin

A deficit in serotonergic neurotransmission has been implicated in impulsivity and poor decision making (Koot et al, 2012). Only few studies have looked at the role of serotonergic systems in gambling. Decreased platelet Monoamine Oxidase – B (MAO-B), increased CSF hydroxylindoleacetic acid (Nordin et al, 2006), and the C/C variant of the Serotonin 2A receptor (Wilson et al, 2012) have been shown in subjects with gambling disorder. A PET imaging study using a Serotonin 1B receptor ligand found higher levels of binding in the anterior cingulate cortex and the ventral striatum, which correlated with scores on the South Oaks Gambling Screen (Potenza et al, 2013). The use of specific serotonin reuptake inhibitor (SSRI) drugs has been found to yield modest improvements in the overall severity of gambling disorders, mainly through reducing impulsivity and improvements in comorbid anxiety or depression (Labuzek et al, 2014).

Norepinephrine

Norepinephrine modulates the physiological response to the state of arousal, which is typically seen during the anticipation of rewards in gambling. It is also involved in decision making when contingencies are unexpectedly changed and alternatives are explored. Inhibition of norepinephrine reuptake using agents such as atomoxetine or reboxetine results in reduced premature responding, especially when task performance is sub - optimal due to demands of the task or high levels of baseline impulsivity.

Preliminary research found that patients with gambling disorder had significantly higher CSF levels of 3-methoxy -4- hydroxyl-phenylglycol (MHPG), which is the final metabolite of norepinephrine (Brown, 1987;

Roy et al, 1989). Meyer et al (2004) also found persistently elevated levels of norepinephrine during a gambling session in patients with gambling disorder in contrast to normal subjects in whom the elevation was found only at the beginning of the gambling session.

Endogenous opioids

Opioid receptors and beta-endorphins have been long known to play an important role in the mesolimbic reward system. The blood levels of beta-endorphins have been found to be higher in subjects with gambling disorder as compared to healthy controls (Shinohara, 1999). Several trials have demonstrated the efficacy of opioid receptor antagonists such as nalmefene and naltrexone in treatment of gambling disorder (Grant et al, 2010).

Neuroimaging studies

There have been many more functional neuroimaging than structural imaging studies in gambling disorder. Functional magnetic resonance imaging (fMRI) paradigms include those that assess response inhibition (Go No-Go, Stroop task) (de Ruiter, 2009; Gourdiaan, 2010; Miedl, 2012), decision making (e.g. Iowa gambling task), gain or loss processing (slot machine tasks with monetary incentive) (Romanczuk-Seiferth, 2015), gambling urges and cue reactivity (Potenza et al, 2003; Crockford et al, 2005; Miedl et al, 2014). Paradigms to assess specific cognitive processes in gambling disorder, such as chasing losses, delay discounting and processing of "near-miss" outcomes have also been developed and studied (Quester et al, 2015).

fMRI studies have revealed differential activation patterns in subjects with gambling disorder as compared to controls. Most studies have indicated hypo-activation of various frontal cortical regions in response to paradigms. However, there is either hypo- or hyper-activation of the sub-cortical, specifically, ventral striatal structures (ventral caudate, nucleus accumbens, etc.) and the findings have varied based on the type of task used, types of rewards given, etc.

Several studies have also analyzed functional connectivity in subjects with gambling disorder in both resting state (Koehler et al, 2013; Jung et al, 2014)) and during task - related activation (Peters et al, 2013; van Hoist et al, 2014). They have shown alterations in connectivity between pre-frontal and striatal structures.

Existing structural neuroimaging studies in gambling, being very few in number, have yielded discrepant findings. No grey matter alterations were found on a whole-brain level in two voxel-based morphometry (VBM) studies (Jousta et al, 2011; Van Hoist et al, 2012). Studies using a region of interest (ROI) analyses have indicated volume alterations in the hippocampus and amygdala (Rahman et al, 2014), larger volumes of the ventral striatum (Koehler et al, 2013), smaller volumes of putamen and thalamus (Fuentes et al, 2015) and grey matter volume reductions in the frontal cortical regions (Zois et al, 2015). A common confounder in these studies has been the co-occurrence of substance use disorders, most commonly alcohol dependence in subjects with gambling disorders, which only few studies controlled for.

fMRI studies have brought about the understanding that the reward system plays a major role, which is very similar to that seen in other addictive disorders. Further research will help elucidate the specific processes involved in gambling disorder.

Genetic factors

Five large twin cohort studies have looked at the concordance rates of gambling disorder and they yielded heritability estimates ranging from 50% (Eisen et al, 1998; Slutske et al, 2010; Vitaro et al, 2014) to 83% (Blanco et al, 2012). Twin studies have also helped understand the degree of genetic overlap of gambling disorder with other psychiatric disorders. The highest degree of shared genetic vulnerability was found to occur with alcohol and other substance use disorders (Slutske et al, 2000; Slutske et al, 2013). Though earlier studies failed to show any overlap between gambling and obsessive compulsive disorder, a recent study (Scherrer et al, 2015) looked at the relationship between sub-classes of obsessive compulsive symptoms with gambling and found that 19.4% of the genetic variance was shared.

Molecular genetic studies, on the other hand, are few. Studies using candidate gene approaches have looked at association between specific variants of gene coding for various dopamine (Lobo et al, 2010; Lim et al, 2012; Fagundo et al, 2014) and serotonin receptors (Wilson et al, 2014), and the COMT gene (Guillot et al, 2015). Two genome-wide association studies (GWAS) (Lind et al, 2015; Lang et al, 2016) did not find any single nucleotide peptides (SNP) loci significantly higher in occurrence for gambling disorder. However these findings were found to overlap with other substance - related and behavioral addictions, which is consistent with findings of imaging studies.

Neurocognitive factors

Inability to curtail a repeated pattern of decision making that ignores long-term negative consequences for immediate rewards is thought to result from certain neurocognitive deficits in gambling disordered patients. Deficits across various domains such as working memory, decision-making and inhibitory control have been found in patients with gambling disorder. The Iowa Gambling Task (IGT) is an instrument widely used to assess decision making, with factors such as uncertainty, and reward and punishment (Bechara et al, 1994). Performance on this task has been found to be consistently impaired in those with gambling disorder.

"Delay discounting", which refers to the under-valuing of rewards that are likely to arrive later, was found to be abnormally high in gamblers (Petry, 2001). These deficits which are known to underlie impulsivity have been replicated across various studies.

Neurophysiological factors

Studies have looked at physiological correlates of the arousal state that occurs during gambling and found differences in those with gambling disorder as compared with healthy controls. An EEG study also reported elevated late positivity to gambling cues, similar to that following positive and negative (non-gambling) emotional pictures (Woling et al, 2011). Two EEG studies also reported *increased* feedback-related negativities in problem gamblers in a blackjack game (wins after high-risk hit decisions) (Hewig et al, 2010) and the Iowa Gambling Task (Oberg et al, 2011). Miedl et al (2012) used delay-discounting and probability-discounting procedures, where gamblers discount delayed rewards but prefer uncertain rewards. Several studies have also looked at various physiological responses (heart rate, electro dermal reactivity, facial electromyography, etc.) to "near-miss" outcomes in those with gambling disorder. (Clark et al, 2012; Sharman et al, 2015; Wu et al, 2015.)

Role of impulsivity and compulsivity

Impulsivity is defined as a predisposition towards rapid, unplanned reactions to either internal or external stimuli without regard for negative consequence. Compulsivity on the other hand, is defined as the performance of repetitive behaviours with the goal of reducing or preventing anxiety or distress, not to provide pleasure or gratification.

The trajectory of addiction disorders has been conceptualized as impulsivity being the key "driving force" early in the course of the disorder but this is progressively transformed to compulsivity. The initial positive reinforcement or reward derived by the use of substance is later replaced by the need to take the substance in order to avoid withdrawal, which is negative reinforcement.

A similar motivational shift is seen to occur in gambling, wherein early gambling is generally associated with reward, and more chronic gambling is driven by stress or by the goal of relieving anxiety (el-Guebaly et al, 2011). In addition to this, people with gambling disorder may indulge in certain superstitious, ritualistic behaviours such as wearing certain clothes and lucky charms, and relying on certain "lucky numbers" for a more favourable outcome (Blaszczynski, 1999). Neurocognitive studies have found higher response perseveration (Frost, 2001) and difficulties in cognitive flexibility (Gourdaain, 2005, Odlaug, 2011). Despite these phenomenological similarities, studies have not demonstrated any increased comorbidity rates of OCD in gambling and vice versa. No family clustering or neurocognitive similarities have been found either.

Psychological factors

Behavioral theories

Behavioral theories, both classic and operant conditioning, can convincingly account for most aspects of gambling disorder. The role of intermittent rewards in the variable-ratio reinforcement schedule has been emphasized. Early wins in this type of reinforcement are known to produce greater persistence in the behaviour, even if the reinforcement ratio is decreased, or the reward is stopped. (Petry, 2005). Intermittent rewards help promote the belief that persisting with the behavior through losses is necessary to receive a reward, and the reward itself presents with a great degree of relief and enjoyment in this scheme. The high levels of autonomic arousal that occurs in anticipation of a reward, is postulated to be one of the main reinforcers of gambling behaviour (Anderson & Brown, 1984; Blaszczynski et al, 1986; Sharpe, 1995)

Cognitive distortions

Certain maladaptive cognitive processes have been consistently reported in various studies of gambling disorder from across the world. In addition to behavioral reinforcement, these cognitive distortions are also thought to play an important role in the development and maintenance of gambling disorder. Some such cognitive distortions are discussed:

1. **Gambler's fallacy** - the belief that completely random events such as the outcome of a coin toss are influenced by recent events. Most relevantly, it is the mistaken belief that a string of unreinforced trials will inevitably lead to a win at some point. Most gamblers believe that a series of recent losses increases the likelihood of a win.
2. **Illusions of control** – By indulging in superstitious behaviours, the disordered gambler thinks s/he has a reliable means of manipulating (controlling) the outcome in their favour.
3. **Magnification of gambling skills** – exaggerated self-confidence in games wherein mere chance plays a bigger role than actual skill
4. **Recall bias** – the tendency to remember and overestimate wins while forgetting about and/or underestimating or rationalizing losses
5. **Inaccurate processing of "near-misses" and "full-misses"** – though both these events are objectively equivalent, gamblers tend to experience "near-misses" as salient events which increase their motivation to play further. Gamblers also may misinterpret "near-misses" as an evidence that they are improving their skills
6. **Chasing losses** – is driven by the faulty belief that wagering more frequently and in larger amounts would help recover lost money

Higher levels of cognitive distortions have been found to predict increased risk of future relapse (Oei & Gordon, 2008). However, it has been noted that cognitive distortions are also seen in normal people who gamble (Miller et al, 2008)

Role of personality factors

The key personality trait that has been found and studied extensively in gambling disorder is impulsivity. Sensation - seeking has been found to be more specific to younger onset and male-gender. A meta-analysis of personality traits (Maclaren et al, 2011) found several traits such as negative urgency, low premeditation, unconscientious disinhibition (low conscientiousness), negative affect and disagreeable disinhibition (low agreeableness). These have been subsumed under the broader spectrum of "externalizing" traits and is yet another commonality shared with substance-related addiction disorders. Also, rates of personality disorders comorbid with gambling disorder have been found to be quite high – 45% (Odlaug et al, 2012) to 71% (Giddens et al, 2012).

Socio-cultural factors

Exposure to and availability of gambling is a pre-requisite for gambling disorder, which are dependent on ecological factors determined by society and culture.

Certain cultures view gambling not only as an acceptable recreational activity, but also as a potential career option. In certain other cultures, the act of gambling is frowned upon as a sinful activity. Hence different cultures have different degrees of exposure and accessibility to gambling. The vast and varying socio - cultural landscape of India results in its population having highly varied exposure to gambling (George et al, 2017).

However epidemiological research has not found a clear link between the exposure to and availability of gambling venues to the prevalence of gambling disorder (LaPlante et al, 2007). Certain researchers have also proposed an "adaptation" hypothesis wherein the early greater exposure to gambling venues may confer a protective role upon certain individuals who may become less likely to develop gambling disorder. (Shaffer et al, 2004)

Several other aspects about one's social setting can also impact gambling behaviours. It has been found that different populations (e.g. adolescents, college students, elderly) tend to have different gambling preferences (Moragas et al, 2015). Studies have found that people from disadvantaged communities such as minorities and lower socio-economic groups are more prone to develop higher levels of gambling pathology (Welte, 2004). Lower academic achievement and unemployment are other social risk factors for gambling disorder (Martins et al, 2012).

Conceptual models

Owing to the multitude of factors described above, there is no single theory that can comprehensively account for all aspects of the development and progression of gambling disorder. However, four important evidence-based conceptual models have been proposed. They include the general theory of addictions (Jacobs, 1986), the pathways model (Blaszczynski & Nower, 2002), the public health model (Korn & Shaffer, 1999) and the cognitive behavioural model (Sharpe, 2002; Raylu 2016).

The general theory of addictions

Developed by Jacobs in 1986, this theory attempted to account for both physiological and psychological factors in the etiology of substance use disorders. Any activity that gives a psychologically vulnerable individual an opportunity to escape pain, fulfill grandiose fantasies and create a new identity will lead to addiction. Addiction to behaviours such as gambling represents a maladaptive coping pattern to deal with distressing emotions and conflicts. In addition it has also been demonstrated that cessation of gambling for a certain period can produce a negative emotional state, akin to a withdrawal state in substance addiction disorders. Over a period of time, the need to gamble with increasing amounts of money to achieve the same excitement also typically occurs in the course of gambling disorder. As previously mentioned, accumulation of evidence over the past two decades has led to the re-classification of Gambling disorder in the DSM5 to the section on addiction disorders.

The "Pathways" model

This model, described by Blaszczynski & Nower (2002), takes into consideration the complex array of etiological factors, along with the heterogeneity related to gambling disorder. This model proposes three main pathways leading to three subtypes of the disorder:

- "Behaviourally conditioned" subtype: This group includes those who initiate gambling for social and recreational reasons but go on to develop problematic patterns of gambling because of their gambling history itself. They are characterized by an absence of pre-morbid psychopathological changes or impaired control over gambling, but simply develop the addiction from conditioning, distorted cognitions and poor decision making associated with frequent gambling. Psychopathology such as anxiety and depression are likely to result as a consequence of the losses due to gambling rather than be the cause in itself. Behavioural conditioning and cognitive distortions are also seen in the other two subtypes, although pre-morbid psychopathological changes are associated.
- "Emotionally vulnerable" subtype: This group has particular vulnerability factors as well as gambling conditioning. For example, in those with pre-morbid anxiety or depression, negative life events such as childhood trauma or poor coping strategies, the act of gambling helps bring relief to negative affective states.

- "Antisocial impulsivist" subtype: Includes those who have high levels of impulsivity and borderline or anti-social personality traits in addition to the previous group's factors. For them gambling serves as a risky and exciting activity. The impulsivity may be explained by certain neuropsychological deficits in domains such as executive functioning, comorbid attention-deficit hyperactivity disorder, substance use disorders etc. which may thus lead to greater gambling severity.

Public health model

This paradigm, initially suggested by Shaffer & Korn (2002) takes into consideration the interaction between three variables: the agent (gambling activity), the host (individual vulnerability) and the environment (accessibility of gambling venues, familial, cultural, societal and legal factors). This model recognizes both the positive outcomes (e.g. socio-economic gains and revenue generation, employment opportunities, etc. generated by gambling) as well as the negative outcomes of gambling and helps guide larger, public health policy making for the prevention and treatment of gambling disorder.

Masserlain, Derevensky & Gupta (2004) have applied this model specifically to gambling behaviours in adolescents and elaborated on specific environmental risk, individual vulnerability and protective factors for gambling disorder.

Cognitive behavioural models

This model proposed by Sharpe & Tarrier (1993) states that individuals are likely to have some vulnerability to develop problem gambling. A variety of situations may trigger the temptation to gamble, including gambling-related stimuli and stress, which they argue may stimulate arousal which is similar to that associated with gambling. The interaction of vulnerability with the format of gambling games is thought to generate associations between arousal and cognitive biases to produce a pattern of persistence with gambling, whether the gambler is winning or losing.

The Sharpe (2002) model takes a similar bio-psycho-social approach and incorporated much of the later research into the previous model. In addition to biological vulnerability factors early big wins or a series of relatively small wins may lead to the development of beliefs around gambling such as the 'gambler's fallacy' (runs of 'bad luck' must be followed by good luck) and an illusion of control over gambling. Internal cues (stress or boredom) and external triggers (gambling-related stimuli) interact to activate arousal associated with gambling leading to "gambling urges". Various other authors have further elaborated upon this model. Raylu et al (2015) incorporated the role of negative emotional states (depression and anxiety in particular) along with maladaptive coping strategies (avoidance coping).

Posited integrated model

Various conceptual frameworks have over the years attempted to integrate all factors which may have a role in the development and persistence of gambling disorder. Fig. 2.1 below illustrates how all these factors may interact in the development of gambling disorder.

Figure 2.1

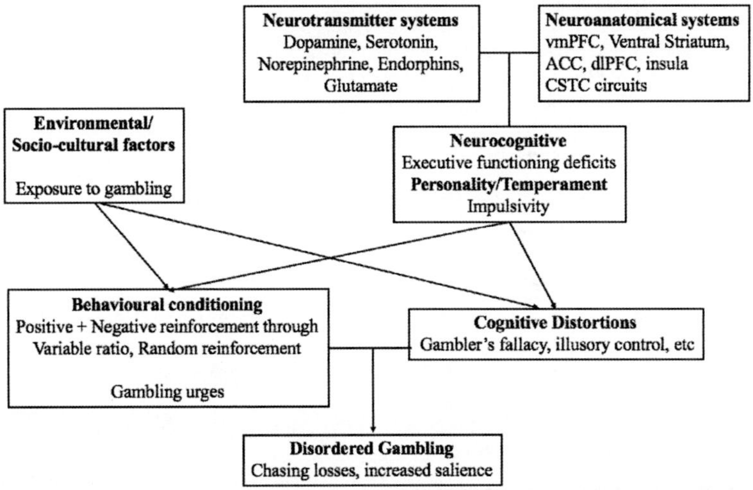

Conclusion

Etiological factors contributing to gambling disorder are multitudinous, and the problem is most likely heterogeneous. A better understanding of factors and conceptual models of gambling disorder will help develop effective and comprehensive management strategies to prevent negative outcomes.

Key points

- Gambling disorder is understood to be a complex, heterogeneous disorder, the etiology of which involves multiples factors (neurobiological, psychological and socio-cultural) interacting with each other.

- Gambling disorder, from a neurobiological perspective, involves a dysfunctional reward system, with diminished top-down control from pre-frontal cortical regions, coupled with excessive drive from sub cortical regions involved in reward processing.
- Noradrenergic, serotonergic, dopaminergic, and opioidergic neurotransmitter systems have been proposed to contribute to arousal/excitement, impulse control, reward/reinforcement, and urges/cravings respectively and their roles have been studied in gambling disorder.
- Inability to curtail a repeated pattern of decision making that ignores long-term negative consequences for immediate rewards are thought to result from neurocognitive deficits across domains such as working memory, decision-making and inhibitory control.
- Behavioral theories, both classic and operant conditioning, can convincingly account for most aspects of gambling disorder: the role of intermittent rewards in the variable-ratio reinforcement schedule has been emphasized.
- Several maladaptive cognitive processes have also been noted.
- There is no single theory that can comprehensively account for all aspects of the development and progression of gambling disorder. However, four important evidence-based conceptual models have been proposed: the general theory of addictions, the pathways model, the public health model and the cognitive behavioural model.

References

American Psychiatric Association. (2013). Diagnostic and statistical manual of mental disorders (DSM-5). Washington, DC. American Psychiatric Association.

Bergh, C., Eklund, T., Södersten, P., Nordin, C. (1997). Altered dopamine function in pathological gambling. *Psychological medicine*. 27(2): 473–475.

Blanco, C., Myers, J., Kendler, K. S. (2012). Gambling, disordered gambling and their association with major depression and substance use: a web-based cohort and twin-sibling study. *Psychological Medicine*, 42(3):497–508.

Blaszczynski, A. (1999). Pathological gambling and obsessive-compulsive spectrum disorders. *Psychological Reports*. 84(1):107–13.

Blaszczynski, A. & Nower, L. (2002). A pathways model of problem and pathological gambling. *Addiction*. 97(5): 487–499.

Clark, L., Crooks, B., Clarke, R., Aitken, M. R. F., Dunn, B. D. (2012). Physiological Responses to Near-Miss Outcomes and Personal Control during Simulated Gambling. *Journal of Gambling Studies*, 28(1):123–37.

Cocker, P. J., Hosking, J. G., Murch, W.S., Clark, L., Winstanley, C. A. (2016). Activation of dopamine D4 receptors within the anterior cingulate cortex enhances the erroneous expectation of reward on a rat slot machine task. *Neuropharmacology*, 105:186–95.

Crockford, D. N., Goodyear, B., Edwards, J., Quickfall, J., el-Guebaly, N. (2005). Cue-Induced Brain Activity in Pathological Gamblers. *Biological Psychiatry*, 58(10):787–95.

Dannon, P. N., Shoenfeld, N., Rosenberg, G., Kertzman, S., Kotler, M. (2010). Pathological gambling: an impulse control disorder? Measurement of impulsivity using neurocognitive tests. *Israel Medical Association Journal*. 1; 12(4):243.

De Ruiter, M. B., Veltman, D. J., Goudriaan, A. E., Oosterlaan, J., Sjoerds, Z., Van Den Brink, W. (2009). Response perseveration and ventral prefrontal sensitivity to reward and

punishment in male problem gamblers and smokers. *Neuropsychopharmacology*, 34(4):1027.
Eisen, S. A., Lin, N., Lyons, M. J., Scherrer, J. F., Griffith, K., True, W. R., Goldberg, J., Tsuang, M. T. (1998). Familial influences on gambling behaviour: an analysis of 3359 twin pairs. *Addiction*, 93(9):1375-84.
Fagundo, A. B., Fernández-Aranda, F., de la Torre, R., Verdejo-García, A., Granero, R., Penelo, E. et al. (2014). Dopamine DRD2/ANKK1 Taq1A and DAT1 VNTR polymorphisms are associated with a cognitive flexibility profile in pathological gamblers. *Journal of Psychopharmacology*, 28(12):1170–7.
el-Guebaly, N., Mudry, T., Zohar, J., Tavares, H., Potenza, M. N. (2012). Compulsive features in behavioural addictions: the case of pathological gambling: Compulsivity in addictions. *Addiction*, 107(10):1726–34.
Fuentes, D., Rzezak, P., Pereira, F. R., Malloy-Diniz, L. F., Santos, L. C., Duran, F. L. et al. (2015). Mapping brain volumetric abnormalities in never-treated pathological gamblers. *Psychiatry Research*, 232(3):208-13.
George, S., Velleman, R., Nadkarni, A. (2017). Gambling in India: Past, present and future, *Asian Journal of Psychiatry*, 26:39-43, http://dx.doi.org/10.1016/j.ajp.2017.01.018.
George, S., Jaisoorya, T.S., Sivasankaran, N.B., Rani, A., Menon, P., Madhavan, R. et al. (2016). A cross-sectional study of problem gambling and its correlates among college students in South India. *British Journal of Psychiatry Open. 2 (3)*:199- 203.
Giddens, J. L., Stefanovics, E., Pilver, C. E., Desai, R., Potenza, M. N. (2012). Pathological gambling severity and co-occurring psychiatric disorders in individuals with and without anxiety disorders in a nationally representative sample. *Psychiatry Research*. 199(1):58–64.
Goudriaan, A.E., Oosterlaan, J., De Beurs, E., Van Den Brink, W. (2006). Neurocognitive functions in pathological gambling: a comparison with alcohol dependence, Tourette syndrome and normal controls. (*Addiction*. 101:534–47 (
Goudriaan, A.E., De Ruiter, M. B., Van Den Brink, W., Oosterlaan, J., Veltman, D. J. (2010). Brain activation patterns associated with cue reactivity and craving in abstinent problem gamblers, heavy smokers and healthy controls: an fMRI study: Neuroimaging cue reactivity in problem gamblers and smokers. *Addiction Biology*. 15(4):491–503.
Grant, J.E., Potenza, M. N., Hollander, E., Cunningham-Williams, R., Nurminen, T., Smits, G. et al. (2006). Multi - centre investigation of the opioid antagonist nalmefene in the treatment of pathological gambling. *American Journal of Psychiatry*, 163(2):303–312.
Grant, J. E., Atmaca, M., Fineberg, N. A. et al. (2014). Impulse control disorders and “behavioural addictions” in the ICD-11. *World Psychiatry*, 13(2):125-127.
Guillot, C. R., Fanning, J. R., Liang, T., Berman, M. E. (2015). COMT Associations with Disordered Gambling and Drinking Measures. *Journal of Gambling Studies*, 31(2):513–24.
Hewig, J., Trippe, R., Hecht, H., Coles, M. G. H., Holroyd, C. B., Miltner, W. H. R. (2007). Decision-making in Blackjack: an electrophysiological analysis. *Cerebral Cortex*, 17(4):865–77.
Hur, J. W., Shin, N. Y., Kim, S. N., Jang, J. H., Choi, J. S., Shin, Y. C., Kwon, J.S. (2012). Do pathological gambling and obsessive-compulsive disorder overlap? A neurocognitive perspective. *CNS Spectr*um, 1; 17(4):207-13.
Koehler, S., Hasselmann, E., Wüstenberg, T., Heinz, A., Romanczuk-Seiferth, N. (2015). Higher volume of ventral striatum and right prefrontal cortex in pathological gambling. *Brain Structure and Function*. 220(1):469–77.

Koot, S., Zoratto, F., Cassano, T., Colangeli, R., Laviola, G., van den Bos, R. et al. (2012). Compromised decision-making and increased gambling proneness following dietary serotonin depletion in rats. *Neuropharmacology*, 62(4):1640–50.

Korn, D. A. & Shaffer, H. J. (1999). Gambling and the Health of the Public: Adopting a Public Health Perspective. *Journal of Gambling Studies*, 15(4):289–365.

Jacobs, D. F. (1986). A general theory of addictions: A new theoretical model. *Journal of Gambling Behaviour*, 1; 2(1):15–31.

Joutsa, J., Johansson, J., Niemelä, S., Ollikainen, A., Hirvonen, M. M., Piepponen, P. et al. (2012). Mesolimbic dopamine release is linked to symptom severity in pathological gambling. *Neuro Image*, 60(4):1992–9.

£abuzek, K., Beil, S., Beil-Gawe³czyk, J., Gabryel, B., Franik, G., Okopień, B. (2014). The latest achievements in the pharmacotherapy of gambling disorder. *Pharmacological Reports*, 66(5):811–20.

Lang, M., Leménager, T., Streit, F., Fauth-Bühler, M., Frank, J., Juraeva, D. et al. (2016). Genome-wide association study of pathological gambling. *European Psychiatry*, 36:38–46.

La Plante, D. A. & Shaffer, H. J. (2007). Understanding the influence of gambling opportunities: Expanding exposure models to include adaptation. *American Journal of Orthopsychiatry*, 77(4):616–23.

Lim, S., Ha, J., Choi, S.W., Kang, S-G., Shin, Y. C. (2012). Association study on pathological gambling and polymorphisms of dopamine D1, D2, D3, and D4 receptor genes in a Korean population. *Journal of Gambling Studies*, 28(3):481–91.

Lind, P. A., Zhu, G., Montgomery, G. W., Madden, P. A. F., Heath, A. C., Martin, N. G. et al. (2013). Genome-wide association study of a quantitative disordered gambling trait: Disordered gambling genetics. *Addiction Biology*, 18(3):511–22.

Linnet, J., Mouridsen, K., Peterson, E., Møller, A., Doudet, D. J., Gjedde, A. (2012). Striatal dopamine release codes uncertainty in pathological gambling. *Psychiatry Research: Neuroimaging*, 204(1):55–60.

Lobo, D. S. S. & Kennedy, J. L. (2009). Genetic aspects of pathological gambling: a complex disorder with shared genetic vulnerabilities. *Addiction*, 104(9):1454–65.

Lobo, D. S. S., Quilty, L. C., Martins, S, S., Tavares, H., Vallada, H., Kennedy, J. L. et al. (2014). Pathological gambling subtypes: A comparison of treatment-seeking and non-treatment-seeking samples from Brazil and Canada. *Addictive Behaviours*, 39(7):1172–5.

Lobo, D. S. S. (2016). Genetic Aspects of Gambling Disorders: Recent Developments and Future Directions. *Current Behavioural Neuroscience Reports*. 2016 Mar; 3(1):58–66.

MacLaren, V. V., Fugelsang, J. A., Harrigan, K. A., Dixon, M. J. (2011). The personality of pathological gamblers: A meta-analysis. *Clinical Psychology Review*, 31(6):1057–67.

Martins, S. S., Storr, C. L., Lee, G. P., Ialongo, N. S. (2013). Environmental Influences Associated with Gambling in Young Adulthood. *Journal of Urban Health*, 90(1):130–40.

Messerlian, C., Derevensky, J., Gupta, R. (2004). A public health perspective for youth gambling. *International Gambling Studies*, 4(2):147–60.

Meyer, G. (2004). Neuroendocrine response to casino gambling in problem gamblers. *Psychoneuroendocrinology*, 29(10):1272–80.

Miedl, S. F., Peters, J., Büchel, C. (2012). Altered neural reward representations in pathological gamblers revealed by delay and probability discounting. *Archives of General Psychiatry*, 69(2):177–186.

Miedl, S. F., Fehr, T., Herrmann, M., Meyer, G. (2014). Risk assessment and reward processing in problem gambling investigated by event-related potentials and fMRI-constrained

source analysis. *BMC Psychiatry* [Internet]. Aug 10; 14.
Miller, N. V. & Currie, S. R. (2008). A Canadian Population Level Analysis of the Roles of Irrational Gambling Cognitions and Risky Gambling Practices as Correlates of Gambling Intensity and Pathological Gambling. *Journal of Gambling Studies*. 24(3):257–74.
Moragas, L., Granero, R., Stinchfield, R., Fernández-Aranda, F., Fröberg, F., Aymamí, N. et al. (2015). Comparative analysis of distinct phenotypes in gambling disorder based on gambling preferences. *BMC Psychiatry* [Internet]. 15(1). Available from: http://bmcpsychiatry.biomedcentral.com/articles/10.1186/s12888-015-0459-0
Nordin, C. & Eklundh, T. (1999). Altered CSF 5-HIAA Disposition in Pathologic Male Gamblers. *CNS Spectrums*. 4(12):25–33.
Oberg, S. A.K., Christie, G. J., Tata, M. S. (2011). Problem gamblers exhibit reward hypersensitivity in medial frontal cortex during gambling. *Neuropsychologia*. 49(13):3768–75.
Ochoa, C., Aymamí, M. N., Gómez-Peña, M., Santamaría, J., Moragas, L., Bove, F., Menchón, J.M. (2011). Effect of executive functioning, decision-making and self-reported impulsivity on the treatment outcome of pathologic gambling. *Journal of Psychiatry & Neuroscience*. 1; 36(3):165.
Odlaug, B.L., Chamberlain, S. R., Kim, S. W., Schreiber, L. R., Grant, J. E. (2011). A neurocognitive comparison of cognitive flexibility and response inhibition in gamblers with varying degrees of clinical severity. *Psychological Medicine*. 1; 41(10):2111-9.
Odlaug, B. L., Schreiber, L. R., Grant, J. E. (2012). Personality disorders and dimensions in pathological gambling. *Journal of Personality Disorders*. 26(3):381–392.
Oei, T. P. S. & Gordon, L. M. (2008). Psychosocial Factors Related to Gambling Abstinence and Relapse in Members of Gamblers Anonymous. *Journal of Gambling Studies*, 24(1):91–105.
Peters, J., Miedl, S. F., Büchel, C. (2013). Elevated Functional Connectivity in a Striatal-Amygdala Circuit in Pathological Gamblers. Gilbert S, editor. *PLoS ONE*, 8(9):e74353.
Petry, N. M. (2001). Pathological gamblers, with and without substance abuse disorders, discount delayed rewards at high rates. *Journal of Abnormal Psychology*, 110(3):482.
Petry, N. M., Stinson, F. S., Grant, B. F. (2005). Comorbidity of DSM-IV pathological gambling and other psychiatric disorders: results from the National Epidemiologic Survey on Alcohol and Related Conditions. *Journal of Clinical Psychiatry*, 66(5):564–74.
Pirritano, D., Plastino, M., Bosco, D., Gallelli, L., Siniscalchi, A., De Sarro, G. (2014). Gambling disorder during dopamine replacement treatment in Parkinson's disease: A Comprehensive Review. *BioMed Research International*, 2014:728038. doi:10.1155/2014/728038.
Potenza, M. N., Steinberg, M. A., Skudlarski, P., Fulbright, R. K., Lacadie, C. M., Wilber, M. K. et al. (2003). Gambling urges in pathological gambling: a functional magnetic resonance imaging study. *Archives of General Psychiatry*. 60(8):828–36.
Potenza, M. N. (2013). How central is dopamine to pathological gambling or gambling disorder? *Frontiers in Behavioural Neuroscience*, 7:206
Potenza, M. N., Walderhaug, E., Henry, S., Gallezot, J. D., Planeta-Wilson, B., Ropchan, J. et al. (2013). Serotonin 1B receptor imaging in pathological gambling. *The World Journal of Biological Psychiatry*. 14(2):139–45.
Quester, S. & Romanczuk-Seiferth, N. (2015). Brain Imaging in Gambling Disorder. *Current Addiction Reports*. 2(3):220–9.

Rahman, A. S., Xu, J., Potenza, M. N. (2014). Hippocampal and amygdalar volumetric differences in pathological gambling: a preliminary study of the associations with the behavioural inhibition system. *Neuropsychopharmacology*, 39(3):738.
Raylu, N., Oei, T. P. S., Loo, J. M. Y., Tsai, J. S. (2016). Testing the Validity of a Cognitive Behavioural Model for Gambling Behaviour. *Journal of Gambling Studies*, 32(2):773–88.
Romanczuk-Seiferth, N., Koehler, S., Dreesen, C., Wüstenberg, T., Heinz, A. (2015). Pathological gambling and alcohol dependence: neural disturbances in reward and loss avoidance processing. *Addiction Biology*, 20(3):557–69.
Scherrer, J. F., Xian, H., Slutske, W. S., Eisen, S. A., Potenza, M...N. (2015). Associations between Obsessive-Compulsive Classes and Pathological Gambling in a National Cohort of Male Twins. *JAMA Psychiatry*, 1; 72(4):342.
Schweighofer, N., Bertin, M., Shishida, K., Okamoto, Y., Tanaka, S. C., Yamawaki, S. et al. (2008). Low-Serotonin Levels Increase Delayed Reward Discounting in Humans. *Journal of Neuroscience*, 28(17):4528–32.
Shaffer, H. J., LaBrie, R. A., LaPlante, D. (2004). Laying the foundation for quantifying regional exposure to social phenomena: considering the case of legalized gambling as a public health toxin. *Psychology of Addictive Behaviours*, 18(1):40–8.
Sharman, S. & Clark, L. (2016). Mixed Emotions to Near-Miss Outcomes: A Psychophysiological Study with Facial Electromyography. *Journal of Gambling Studies*, 32(3):823–34.
Sharpe L, Tarrier N. (1993). Towards a cognitive-behavioural theory of problem gambling. *British Journal of Psychiatry* 1; 162(3):407–12.
Sharpe, L. (2002). A reformulated cognitive-behavioural model of problem gambling. A biopsychosocial perspective. *Clinical Psychology Review*; 22(1):1–25.
Shinohara, K., Yanagisawa, A., Kagota, Y., Gomi, A., Nemoto, K., Moriya, E., et al. (1999). Physiological changes in Pachinko players; beta-endorphin, catecholamines, immune system substances and heart rate. *Applied Human Science*, 18(2):37–42.
Slutske, W. S., Zhu, G., Meier, M. H., Martin, N. G. et al. (2010). Genetic and environmental influences on disordered gambling in men and women. *Archives of General Psychiatry*, 67(6):624–630.
Slutske, W. S., Ellingson, J. M., Richmond-Rakerd, L. S., Zhu, G., Martin, N.G. (2013). Shared Genetic Vulnerability for Disordered Gambling and Alcohol Use Disorder in Men and Women: Evidence from a National Community-Based Australian Twin Study. *Twin Research and Human Genetics*, 16(2):525–34.
Steeve, T. D. L., Miyasaki, J., Zurowski, M., Lang, A. E., Pellecchia, G., Van Eimeren, T. et al. (2009). Increased striatal dopamine release in Parkinsonian patients with pathological gambling: a [11C] raclopride PET study. *Brain*, 132(5):1376–85.
van Holst, R. J., van den Brink, W., Veltman, D. J., Goudriaan, A. E. (2010). Brain Imaging Studies in Pathological Gambling. *Current Psychiatry Reports*, 12(5):418–25.
van Holst, R. J., van den Brink, W., Veltman, D. J., Goudriaan, A. E. (2010). Why gamblers fail to win: a review of cognitive and neuroimaging findings (in pathological gambling. *Neuroscience and Biobehavioural Reviews*, 34:87–107
van Holst, R. J., de Ruiter, M. B., van den Brink, W., Veltman, D. J., Goudriaan, A. E. (2012). A voxel-based morphometry study comparing problem gamblers, alcohol abusers, and healthy controls. *Drug and Alcohol Dependence*, 124(1–2):142–8.

Vitaro, F., Hartl, A. C., Brendgen, M., Laursen, B., Dionne, G., Boivin, M. (2014). Genetic and environmental influences on gambling and substance use in early adolescence. *Behavioural Genetics*, 44(4):347–55.
Welte, J. W., Barnes, G. M., Wieczorek, W. F., Tidwell, M. C. O., Parker, J.C. (2004). Risk factors for pathological gambling. *Addictive Behaviours*, 29(2):323–35.
Wilson, D., da Silva Lobo, D. S., Tavares, H., Gentil, V., Vallada, H. (2013). Family-Based Association Analysis of Serotonin Genes in Pathological Gambling Disorder: Evidence of Vulnerability Risk in the 5HT-2A Receptor Gene. *Journal of Molecular Neur oscience*, 49(3):550–3.
Wölfling, K., Mörsen, C. P., Duven, E., Albrecht, U., Grüsser, S. M., Flor, H. (2011). To gamble or not to gamble: at risk for craving and relapse—learned motivated attention in pathological gambling. *Biological Psychology*, 87(2):275–81.
Wu, Y., Van Dijk, E., Aitken, M., Clark, L. (2016). Missed losses loom larger than missed gains: Electro dermal reactivity to decision choices and outcomes in a gambling task. *Cognitive, Affective, & Behavioural Neuroscience*, 16(2):353–61.
Zois, E., Kiefer, F., Lemenager, T., Vollstädt-Klein, S., Mann, K., Fauth-Bühler, M. (2017). Frontal cortex grey matter volume alterations in pathological gambling occur independently from substance use disorder: Frontal cortex and addiction. *Addiction Biology*, 22(3):864–72.

Chapter 3

Gambling laws in India

George Johnson

Introduction

Gambling is recognized as a legitimate recreational activity and has always been a popular pastime in India. While for most people gambling remains a leisure activity, for some, it can become problematic with significant disruption to personal, family or recreational pursuits. Across the world, most governments have recognised the disruptive potential of unbridled gambling and have formulated laws to restrict and regulate gambling practices.

In India, legislative attempts to restrict gambling have been in force since 1867, with the implementation of *The Public Gambling Act*(Act 3 of 1867) in British - ruled India. This chapter will review the various gambling laws in India both at the state and central levels. As state legislative processes vary across the 29 India states, gambling laws in Kerala and Goa (two states with relatively liberal gambling laws) have been selected to discuss their specific legislations including the social/administrative background/ rationale for the legislations across decades. This will help understand the complexity of legal processes. Further, this overview of gambling laws has been contextualized with an initial brief description of the law making processes followed in India, which aims to improve the readers' understanding of gambling laws in the country.

Constitution and the law making process in India

Constitution of India is the supreme law of India and any enactment which is made by the Parliament or the State Legislature has to stand the test of constitutionality. Or in other words, if a law is passed by the Parliament and if the President gives assent, and if there are certain provisions of the Act which are not in tune with the Constitution, then those provisions of the Act can be declared as unconstitutional either by the Supreme Court or by the High Court – and this is in essence the test of constitutionality.

Power of the Government in enforcing provisions of the enactment

Even though a legislation is enacted, Government has the prerogative to decide as to which of the provisions of the Act are to be enforced and when they need to be enforced. Take for example the recent enactment on 'Juvenile Justice.' The 'Juvenile Justice (Care and Protection of Children) Act 2015' (Act No 2 of 2016 http://www.indiacode.nic.in/acts-in-pdf/2016/201602.pdf) was passed by both houses of Parliament, the Lok Sabha and the Rajya Sabha in 2015. Assent of the President was also obtained. However, the provisions of the enactment were only enforced from 15th of January 2016. There can be cases in which certain provisions of the enactment can be enforced initially, and after a certain period rest of the provisions can be enforced. Clarity of the above is essential to understand the law making process in India.

Power of the central and state governments in enacting laws

As noted earlier, laws are made by virtue of the power given under the Constitution of India. Both the Government of India (Union) and individual States can enact laws. Logically, a question arises here - in which areas can the Union and the State/ States enact laws? And the answer lies in understanding Article 246 of the Constitution of India (http://lawmin.nic.in/olwing/coi/coi-english/coi-4March2016.pdf). As per the said provision, the Union has exclusive power to enact laws on subjects/in areas which are stated in List 1 of the Seventh Schedule of the Constitution; which means on topics like defence, navy, arms, firearms etc. only the Parliament can make laws. For subjects that are stated in List II of Seventh Schedule, State governments have exclusive power to enact laws. So, for enacting laws on public order, police, public health and intoxicating liquors, etc. only the State government has the power to enact laws. For subjects that are included in List III, both the Union as well as States have the power to enact laws.

Definitions of terms

Often, the words "gaming", "gambling", 'betting' and 'wagering' are used synonymously and interchangeably in legal lexicon. In the Black Law Dictionary 10th Edition (Garner, 2009) there is no precise definition given for the word 'gaming' but on page 793, against the meaning of 'gaming', a cross reference is made to the word gambling. And 'gambling' is defined as an "act of risking something of value, especially money, on a chance to win a prize". The expression "gaming" can be interpreted as equivalent to "playing a game". Gaming generally denotes playing any game whether of chance or skill (or mixed chance and skill) for money or monies worth (Dyson v. Mason, 1889 22 QBD 351).

Gambling laws

As far as the subject/area of gambling and betting laws are concerned, it falls under List II of the State list in the 7th Schedule of the Constitution of India, which means the concerned State/s have the sole power to enact laws that regulate gambling and betting. Thus, if any State feels that it needs more stringent laws, then the said State is free to enact a law which stringently regulates gambling and betting in that State.

The Public Gambling Act 1867

This law, the Public Gambling Act of 1867, remains the single most important law that regulates gambling in India. It was passed by the British during their rule of India, with a view to regulate and discourage gambling on games of chance. Its aim was to provide for the punishment of public gambling and the keeping of common gaming houses in certain parts of British-ruled India (the United Provinces, East Punjab, Delhi and the Central Provinces). It restricted most forms of gambling but clearly differentiated games of pure chance such as Satta or numbers gambling (which was made illegal) from games of skill and not just mere chance such as horse racing (which was made legal). However the Act does not define gaming.

In this Act, "common gaming house" means any house, walled enclosure, room or place in which cards, dice, tables or other instruments of gaming are kept or used for the profit or gain of the person owning, occupying, using or keeping such house, enclosure, room or place, whether by way of charge for the use of the instruments of gaming, or of the house, enclosure, room or place or otherwise howsoever" (http://www.sangrurpolice.in/wp-content/themes/intrepidity/images/actrule/publicGamblingAct1867.pdf).

The Public Gambling Act 1867 has 18 Sections and there are provisions for keeping or having charge of gaming houses. Section 4 of the enactment provides for penalty for being found in the gaming house and Section 5 gives power to the police to enter the gaming house for the purpose of conducting a search. Section 7 of the enactment provides for penalty on a person being arrested for giving false name and address. Section 12 of the enactment is ambiguous – it exempts certain games and thus by virtue of the said provision, the enactment does not apply to any game of mere skill, where it is played. Mere skill means pure skill and nothing else/no element of chance. There are games in which the outcome (win/lose) of the game is determined by pure/mere chance and not by any degree of skill. Where a game is one of chance and not skill, provisions of the enactment are attracted. There may be an element of difficulty/ambiguity in the case of certain games to decide whether it is a game of chance or skill. Because in such games elements of chance and skill may coexist. A test in such cases is to assess whether the dominating element is of skill or of chance. Hence the question as to whether the game would come under the ambit of the enactment would depend upon the facts and circumstances of the case. Section 13 of the Act mentions gaming and talks about putting birds and animals for fight in public streets. By virtue of Section 13, a police officer, without a warrant, can arrest a person who is found playing for money or for other valuable things and the said police officer can also arrest in case where birds or animals are made to fight in public or within limits prescribed. Section 14 of the enactment confers powers to the magistrate to try such offences where they are committed. Section 16 is a rewarding section by which informers are rewarded for bringing the offence to the notice of the concerned authorities. As per Section 16 of the enactment, portion of the fine or money that is confiscated can be paid to the informer.

Thus the provisions of the Public Gambling Act are aimed at curbing the act of gaming and gambling in India.

Gambling laws in Indian states

The Centre has devolved exclusive powers to individual states to make necessary amendments to the 1867 Act, as they deem fit, to regulate or de-regulate gambling or to deem what types of gambling are legal or illegal within their own state boundaries. Or in other words, there are provisions in the Act by which individual states are given liberty to adopt whole or part of the enactment for being implemented in their respective states.

As per these provisions, individual states have made amendments from time to time. Currently, lotteries are legal in 13 of the 29 Indian states and 5 Union territories, horse racing is legal only in six states and casinos are legal only in two states (Goa and Sikkim).

Gambling laws in the state of Kerala

This section will look at the amendments followed in the state of Kerala where the Public Gambling Act 1967 has been amended extensively. The state of Kerala has been selected as it was the first state in India to start a state-run lottery, in 1967. The lottery remains extremely popular and is an important revenue generator. But the mid-90s saw an explosion of on-line lottery which led to significant revenue losses and made the government respond with further amendments to ensure its monopoly. The example of Kerala will help understand the constitutional, administrative and public discourse which has shaped gambling laws in individual Indian states after independence.

The first major change in the *The Public Gambling Act 1867* was the enactment of Kerala Gaming Act (Act 20 of 1960) – (Published in Kerala Gazette Extraordinary dt.11/10/1960).This Act provides for punishment for gaming and keeping of common houses in the state of Kerala. The statements of objects and reasoning of Gaming Act are as follows:

"*The laws in for ce in the differ ent areas of the S tate providing for the punishment of public gambling and the keeping of common gaming houses are, the Travancore Public Gambling Act, III of 1071, the Cochin Public Gambling Act, IV of 1082 and the Madras Gaming Act, 1930 (III of 1930). It is consider ed necessary to have a uniform legislation for the whole S tate. Hence this Bill. "(Pub. In K. G . Ex. No. 40 dt. 15/06/1960*)

This Act was amended for the last time in 2005 (Act 19 of 2005, http://www.sherrylegal.com/articles/6/Gaming%20Act%20-%20Kerala%20Gaming%20Act%202005.pdf) by which permitting marketing and selling online lotteries were also brought under the ambit of the Kerala Gaming Act.

There was a time, when online lotteries and lotteries of other states were allowed to be sold in Kerala. At that time there were no effective laws or regulations on the sale of online lotteries. In spite of having the Lotteries Regulations Act, many online lotteries like "Play win" became very popular in Kerala. As these online lotteries were registered outside Kerala, the revenue generated also 'flowed' to other states. Hence the authorities made suitable amendments in the Kerala Gaming Act, making playing or participating in online lotteries an offence.

As per the Kerala Gaming Amendment Act of 2005 (Act 19 of 2005), the sale of online lotteries was banned. Please have a look at Section 2(b) of the Act (post amendment)

2(b) "*Gaming*" means wagering or betting, or gambling, which includes the organizing, conducting, promoting, marketing or selling of on-line lotteries; but does not include paper lotteries organized, conducted or promoted by any state government or the central government.

Explanation 1: For the purpose of this definition, wagering or betting shall be deemed to comprise the collection or soliciting of bets, the receipt or distribution of winnings or prizes in money or otherwise, in respect of any wager or bet, or any act which is intended to aid or facilitate wagering or betting or such collection, soliciting, receipt or distribution;

Explanation 2: For the purpose of this definition, gambling shall be deemed to comprise the conduct of on-line lotteries, by electronic device including computers, computer peripherals and other equipment for operating on-line lottery systems, lottery terminals, etc., through common gaming houses by selection of numbers or series of numbers which may be predetermined, instantly determined, pre-printed or pre-designed and whereby one or more of such participants who selected a specific number or series of numbers may or may not be declared as winners and rewarded with pre-determined, instantly determined, Pre-printed or pre-designed winnings or prizes in the form of money or otherwise.

Further, Clause c, d, e and f were also inserted by the amendment Act of 2005.

(c) "*Instruments of gaming*" include any article or any electronic devices including computers and computer peripherals and other equipment for operating on-line lottery systems, on-line lottery terminals etc. used or intended to be used as a subject or means of, or for the purpose of carrying on or facilitating or in connection with gaming any books, lists, tickets, forms or other documents used or intended to be used as a register or record or evidence of gaming, the proceeds of any gaming, and any winnings or prizes in money or otherwise, distributed or intended to be distributed in respect of any gaming.

(d) "*On-line lottery*" means a system of gambling organized, conducted, promoted, marketed, or sold through electronic devices including computers, computer peripherals and other equipment for operating on-line lottery systems, lottery terminals etc. where the information about the player's choice of any particular number or combination of numbers etc. is simultaneously registered with the central computer server which assigns a unique number to verify the validity.

(e) "*On-line lottery terminal*" means a terminal connected to a central computer server where on-line lottery tickets are marketed or sold in retail in common gaming houses.

(f) "*Paper lottery*" means any lottery other than on-line lottery.

The Kerala Gaming Act provides for penalties for conducting gambling. Section 3 of the enactment states that where the offence relates to online lotteries, punishment can be up to 3 years' imprisonment and a fine of Rs. 50000. Section 4 of the enactment provides for penalty for being found in a gaming house and the penalty may be extended to a fine of Rs.500 or imprisonment which may extend to a period of one month. As per the provisions of the Act, a sub inspector of police or the concerned magistrate can enter into the place and conduct a search, if there are reasons to believe that gambling and/or gaming is being carried out.

Provisions similar to Public Gambling Act 1867 are also there in the Kerala Gaming Act where by the provisions of the Kerala Gaming Act are not made applicable in cases where the game is played by way of skill. Provisions of Public Gambling Act and Kerala Gaming Act are more or less similar except for the fact that Kerala Gaming Act has provisions to curb online gaming and lottery. As stated above, laws relating to gambling is a state subject and only state governments have the power under the Constitution of India to enact laws relating to gambling. Hence provisions of the Public Gambling Act cannot be extended to the state of Kerala and the said provisions are otiose as far as State of Kerala is concerned. In other words, no police officer or authorities under the Public Gambling Act can enforce any of the provisions of the Public Gambling Act outside the state of Kerala.

It is worthwhile to note here that as per list II of the 7th Schedule of the Constitution of India, individual state governments are given the power to levy appropriate fees and taxes for betting and gambling

The sale of lotteries in Kerala is regulated by the Lotteries Regulation Act, 1998. The enactment gives powers to the state government to conduct lotteries. Thus the sale and conduct of lotteries can be a source of revenue for the government. The Act prohibits such sale and conduct of lotteries by any private individual. In a particular state, the said state government is free to prohibit sale of lotteries conducted by other states. When Kerala government realized that much of the revenue which the state government could have otherwise earned was lost, the government banned the sale and promotion of all such lotteries in Kerala in 2005.

Gambling laws in Goa

The Provisions in Goa, Daman & Diu Public Gambling Act, 1976 are in Pari Materia to the Central Act i.e. Public Gambling Act, 1867. The Goa, Daman & Diu Public Gambling Act 1976, has been subjected to several amendments so as to ensure that adequate punishment is provided for offences under the Act.

Section 3 of the Goa, Daman & Diu Public Gambling Act 1976 prescribes punishment for keeping common gaming houses. Section 3 of the Act provides punishment with imprisonment for a term which may extend up to 3 years and also with a fine which may extend to 5000 rupees. Section 4 of the Act mentions punishment for gaming in common gaming houses. For a first offence, the imprisonment shall be not less than 3 months and fine shall be not less than 2500 rupees. For a second offence imprisonment shall not be less than 6 months and fine shall not be less than 3000 rupees. For the third and subsequent offences, imprisonment shall not be less than 1 year and fine shall not be less than 5000 rupees. Section 5 authorizes any police officer not below the rank of a head constable of police to enter any house, room or place where he has reasons to believe that the said room or place is used as common gaming house. Section 12 of the Act gives power to a police officer not below the rank of a sub inspector of police to arrest without warrant any person who prints, publishes, sells, distributes or in any other manner circulates in newspaper news or in any other document or any news or information which aids to encourage or facilitate gaming. Section 13A of the Act dilutes rigors of the Act. The said provision permits the Government to give authorization to five star hotels and to vessels on board to conduct games, and electronic amusement/slot machines. There has been total exclusion of the provisions of the Act as far as games allowed in five star hotels are concerned. It is clear from Section 18 of the Act that the State enactments prevail over the Central enactments.

A case for further de-regulation?

Kerala state lotteries generate significant revenue for the government, they provide employment for many people, and some of its funds are used for charitable and public purposes. In view of these arguments, there is perhaps a case for less stringent curbs on at least certain forms of gambling within Kerala. Perhaps from a legal perspective, if suitable amendments are carried out to the Gaming Act, gambling can be run as a business (by the state) promoting 'responsible' gambling while protecting the vulnerable from the adverse effects of gambling. There can be provisions in law whereby sufficient checks and balances are in place to ensure this.

Conclusion

In summary, gambling remains a mostly illegal activity in India. The Public Gambling Act 1867, has at its core an intention to curb most forms of gambling, especially games of mere chance. States in India have the power, either to enact or to make suitable amendments in the laws relating to gambling or gaming and to ban or de-regulate gambling within their boundaries. However, considering that gambling remains immensely popular and in a changing world of greater exposure to online gambling and sport betting, it is perhaps time to re-visit existing legal provisions to ensure that the laws are more relevant to the present.

Key points

- In India, legislative attempts to restrict gambling have been in force since 1867, with the implementation of The Public Gambling Act in British - ruled India.
- To this day, the Public Gambling Act of 1867 remains the single most important law that regulates gambling in India.
- The Centre has devolved exclusive powers to individual states to make necessary amendments to the 1867 Act, as they deem fit, to regulate or de-regulate gambling or to deem what types of gambling are legal or illegal within their own state boundaries.
- The only legal forms of gambling in India are state-run lotteries (only in some states), horse racing (six states), rummy card games and casinos (in two states). Lotteries are legal in only 12 states and 5 Union territories but banned in 17 states.
- Gambling remains a mostly illegal activity in India although gambling is very popular in India.
- It is time to re-visit existing legal provisions to ensure that gambling laws are more relevant to the present.

References

Garner, B.A. (2009). The Black Law Dictionary 10th Edition. Thomson West Publishers, USA.

Kerala Gaming Act, 1960 [Internet]. Sherry Legal Consultants. [cited 2018 January 2]. Available from: http://www.sherrylegal.com/articles/6/Gaming%20Act%20-%20Kerala%20Gaming%20Act%202005.pdf

The Public Gambling Act, 1867 [Internet]. Sangrur Police; [cited 2018 January 2]. Available from: http://www.sangrurpolice.in/wp-content/themes/intrepidity/images/actrule/publicGamblingAct1867.pdf

The Lotteries (Regulation) Act, 1998 [Internet]. Government of Kerala, India: [cited 2018 January 2]. Available from: https://www.kerala.gov.in/documents/10180/5604f6ba-b066-4eb0-ac8b-9718c6efd636

Chapter 4

Illegal gambling in India and a case for legal reform

Neeraj Chauhan

Introduction

Gambling in India is as old as civilization itself. Ancient texts such as *Rig Veda* dating back to circa 4000-1500 BC have spoken about the ills of gambling. Even the ancient Sanskrit epic *Mahabharata*, written by Vyasa, describes Yudhisthira's love for the game of dice at length (Bhide, 2007). Gambling in India is not limited to dice games. Other ancient texts too have depicted gambling activities such as betting on animal fights, races and sport.

Gambling continued to prevail in British - ruled India. During the 18th and 19th centuries, numbers gambling colloquially called *Satta* was very popular. Bets were made on things ranging from the price of cotton and gold to opium to other commodities. This practice was viewed adversely by the British and in the latter half of the 19th century, they legislated against the practice of gambling citing reasons such as bankruptcy, flesh trade and general moral decline.

Finally, in 1867, The Public Gambling Act was enacted in India with the goal of restricting various forms of gambling. After independence, gambling was placed under the Seventh schedule, List II, thereby making it a State subject. All the gambling - related state laws have been formulated in line with the principal central Act leaving little room for broadening of its scope. At present, only two states—Goa and Sikkim have permitted casinos, and lotteries are permitted only in 13of the 29 states in India and five Union Territories. But it appears that restrictions have not affected the popularity of gambling: the National Crime Records Bureau reported over 7 lakh cases being registered under The Public Gambling Act 1867 between 2010 and 2015 (Ministry of Home Affairs, 2015).

Illegal gambling activities and their economic impact

While legal gambling is limited to certain games, a range of gambling activities continues to be illegal but popular in India. Gambling games like Matka (betting on two-three digit numbers), Satta, and betting on outcome of elections, political events and on sports are widespread. As per the income tax department of India, these funds are often transferred through hawala transactions. According to a news report published in The Independent in 2017, the Indian gambling market is estimated to be worth about 60 billion dollars per year. Moreover, each year, the total value of bets waged in India in the black market is estimated to be around 40 billion dollars, out of which more than half is bet on cricket (The Independent, 2017).

Over the years, the illegal gambling market in India has led to the setting up of a parallel economy, which is also purportedly funding international crime syndicates involved in drug trafficking and terror-related activities. The illegal gambling market takes money from poor people, who in the hope of making easy money overlook the risks, and transfer it to a few gambling operators. The prospect of making a quick buck is lucrative for some people and this has led to more people indulging in illegal betting which in turn contributes to overall economic instability (Palai et al, 2006).

Betting on/in sport

Betting on sport, especially cricket is the most common form of illegal gambling in India. It is estimated that the global legal sports betting market is worth more than 400 billion dollars (The Hindustan Times, 2017).

Cricket is the most loved, played and watched sport in India. So it follows that a game that interests a country of 1.3 billion people would attract enormous amounts of money to its betting market. With the setting up of the Indian Premier League and International cricket T20 World cup, there has been a reported spurt on betting on cricket (Benegal, 2013). Since betting on cricket remains illegal all over India it is possible to make exact estimates of the size of the betting market. In 2016, a news report published in the Hindustan Times estimated that bets worth 200 million dollars were placed on every one-day international match played by the Indian cricket team.

This ginormous illegal betting market has also given rise to rigging of cricket matches. In the year 2000 the biggest match-fixing scandal in cricket was exposed: the then South African cricket team captain, Wessell Johannes Cronje ("Hansie Cronje" or "Cronje") confessed to providing information to an Indian bookie to rig a match in exchange for money. The Indian police, who were investigating the case, released transcripts of the telephonic conversations between Cronje and an Indian Businessman where it was revealed that several cricket matches played between South Africa and India were fixed through illegal betting (Cricinfo, 2017).

In 2010, three of Pakistan's national cricket players were prosecuted by cricket's world governing body, the International Cricket Council (ICC) for spot - fixing. The three players, including Pakistan's cricket team captain Salman Butt, were held guilty of corruption for taking money from an Indian bookie to throw no balls and wide balls in a cricket test match. All three were banned from playing cricket for varying durations (Cricinfo, 2017). Subsequently, the court of United Kingdom also sentenced them to jail terms after convicting them in the case (BBC News, 2017).

Even though both the above - mentioned cases involved cricketers of countries other than India, they both involved Indian bookmakers. According to the Central Bureau of Investigation, India is the 'ground zero' for cricket betting and the illegal gambling market has flourished since India won the cricket world cup in 1983 (International Law Review, 2017).

Explaining how betting works in cricket, an Indian bookie, who was interviewed by the author (personal communication), said-

"One of the teams is the favourite to win and other is not. People can place bets on either of the teams. Let's take for example an India vs. Bangladesh cricket match in India. The betting rates would be 30 to 32 paise, which means if someone places a bet of Rs. 10,000 on India, and India wins, he will get Rs. 13,000. But if Bangladesh wins, he will lose his principal amount (Rs. 10,000). There are 10 over bets in T-20 (twenty over matches) cricket matches and in fifty over matches, the bets go on for any number of overs. Betting depends on which team is stronger, pitch conditions, and is it a home or away match? and so on. The person who puts bet and runs it called Dabba, gets a permanent commission of Rs. 5,000 to Rs. 10,000 per month from regular customers. Bets can be placed over the phone or in person."

When asked about the extent of illegal betting on cricket in India, he said, "Nobody has an idea but the business runs in several lakh crore rupees. And I can tell you that there is a bookie in every street."

Gambling and crime in India

While gambling is illegal in India and indulging in it is a criminal offence, this illegal and hence unregulated market has become a funding source for other criminal activities. For instance, the hawala market in India thrives mostly on money generated from high-level betting. In 2013, Delhi Police, in its charge sheet in the Indian Premier League (IPL) spot-fixing scandal had linked the illegal betting business directly to India's most wanted criminal – underworld don Dawood Ibrahim (Livemint, 2013). He is also listed as a 'global terrorist' in the UN Sanctions list. A Delhi Police investigation report on Dawood Company's illegal betting racket stated that "it is Dawood Ibrahim Kaskar who ultimately controls the betting racket through his associates in India." The entire international betting syndicate is controlled through a chain of hawala operators. There are established bookies in chain of commands who place bets on behalf of punters and who involve cricketers to act as per their command in lieu of money".

Investigations revealed that the money earned in cricket betting is being used in other illegal activities of D Company. "The bigger fortune is earned by international syndicate (referring to D Company men), which controls the rate as well as direction of gambling. The illegal proceeds of this betting syndicate get invested in various economic activities," the report further stated.

At a more individual level, there have been documented instances where to further the habit of betting, an individual has committed other crimes. For instance, in 2016, the Crime Branch of Delhi police arrested a 35-year old man in an alleged espionage racket where he reportedly passed on confidential information to Pakistan immigration officers during their visit to New Delhi. When probed, it was revealed that the accused had heavy debts due to his habit of betting on cricket matches and to clear those debts he was lured into spying (Times of India, 2016). During his interrogation, Ashok (name changed) confessed that he had heavy debts and borrowed money from small traders. As the owner of a small grocery store, Ashok was unable to pay off his debt which ran into lakhs of rupees.

Newer trends in gambling

According to a report titled "Global Gambling and Betting Market 2015" published by the Hamburg - based business intelligence company yStats.com (2015), the last decade and half has witnessed the advent and expansion of online gambling. Online gambling is on a steady rise with higher internet penetration, faster connectivity and the smart phone boom. This report has forecast that online gambling will see a ten percent growth rate over the next four years. Given a boom in online gaming, several countries are moving towards regulating this and adopting stringent rules as revenues and concerns continue to grow. In India, while online gambling is still at a nascent stage, increasing penetration and speed of internet, and the easy accessibility to gambling opportunities are likely to lead to an increase in both rates of gambling participation and problem gambling. This can lead to a further boom in the already existing illegal gambling market.

Gambling legislation in India: pitfalls and suggestions

Gambling in India, as mentioned earlier, is still governed by the 150-year-old 'The Public Gambling Act 1867'. The Act, which has not been amended to keep pace with modern times, is ambivalent in nature. For instance, the Act makes a clear distinction between games of skill and games of chance, and applies only to games of chance. Section 12 of the Act states, "Act not to apply to certain games. Nothing in the foregoing provisions of this Act contained shall be held to apply to any game of mere skill wherever played." Although what constitutes a game of skill or gambling is not defined in the Act, The Supreme Court of India in its 1996 judgment on the matter '*Dr. K.R. Lakshmanan vs State Of Tamil Nadu and Another*' elaborated upon it (Indiankanoon.org, 2017). The Supreme Court stated that "those competitions in which success depended on substantial degree of skill were not gambling and despite there being an element of chance if a game is preponderantly a game of skill it would nevertheless be a game of mere skill". To explain a game of skill, the court only analyzed horse racing on the grounds that it is a sport where the participant has to have knowledge of the breed of horse, competence of the jockey, training, etc. Therefore, horse racing was considered as a game of skill and hence, was outside the ambit of the Act. Cricket, consequently, according to the Supreme Court's explanation would have come under the purview of game of skill, but the lack of a proper definition of which games come under the purview of 'game of skill' under the Act, betting on all games including cricket is still illegal in India. Considering the nature and scope of cricket in India, banning gambling on this particular sport leaves it susceptible to corruption. In order to minimize corruption and regulate the sport, council chief of the International Cricket Council has urged India to legalize gambling (Emory International Law Review, 2017).

Though, most legal experts agree that gambling legislation in India is in urgent need of revision there is lack of consensus on what needs to be done. Gambling is a state subject under the constitution of India and with individual states legislating, the current laws around gambling across states are non-uniform.

Thus, governments of some states allow and promote lotteries, and betting on horse races, and see it as a potential revenue generator while in most other states it is illegal. Explaining why there is no clear definition of illegal gambling in India, former Delhi police commissioner Neeraj Kumar, who is currently the chief advisor of the Board of Control of Cricket in India's (BCCI) Anti-Corruption & Security Unit (ACSU), said (personal communication),

"Gambling regulation should come under the remit of the government of India. It should not be left to individual states. There are major problems associated with gambling. Many people have committed suicide because they lost money gambling. At the time of lottery also, there were many suicides. An investigation was done by Delhi Police's Crime branch in 1992-1993, which led to the banning of lotteries. We had prepared findings on lottery and submitted to the Supreme Court. Based on that, lottery was banned. And even there we had found that a number of suicides were taking place because of lotteries. And most of these people who ended their lives were extremely poor. Another important thing which most people don't know is that terrorism in Manipur started because of lotteries."

When asked why there are no robust laws on match-fixing, gambling, etc. in India and why the government isn't looking to legalize it anytime soon, Kumar, who had also unearthed the spot-fixing scandal in Indian Premier League in 2013 said,

"The Sports bill, which was introduced by the Congress in 2013, is still pending. That is because it is not a priority and a certain section of powerful people and lobbies will be adversely affected by the Bill. This lobby will do anything for it not to happen. But for poor people, there is no cohesive group in India which wants to work on it. So this legislation will remain pending. At the same time, countries like New Zealand, Australia, South Africa, they have very strong laws on betting."

Indeed, the penalties for offences committed under the Public Gambling Act are also archaic and have lost their significance today. For instance, the penalty for association with a common gaming house, or conducting the business of a gaming house is a fine of Rs. 200 or a three - month jail term. So too, any person who is found in the gaming house can be fined up to Rs. 100 or sentenced to one month in jail.

Online gambling still unregulated in India

Out of the three billion internet users in the world, 277 million are currently in India, making it the world's second largest mass audience driven by technology (Deccan Chronicle, 2017). The internet boom in India has gone beyond e-commerce, advertising and social media. The online betting market and its virtual nature make it easier for illegal gambling to flourish despite it being banned in India. The law that governs the internet in India is the Information Technology Act, 2000 (IT) (Ministry of Law, Justice and Company Affairs, Government of India 2000). This legislation was enacted 17 years ago, at a time when the use of internet in India was limited. Despite the manifold increase in the number of internet users in India since 2000, the law remains unchanged. The IT Act does not cover online betting in its scope, leaving the online betting market largely unregulated. Explaining scope and extent of online betting in India, Kumar said (personal communication)

"There are many websites like *betfair.com* where online betting is allowed. Their servers and IP addresses are based abroad and so it's difficult to trace them. But I would say that first we should have a legal structure for betting, and then slowly everything will come into that including online betting. We need to recognize the magnitude of the problem. In India, cricket is hugely popular, and other sports are also catching up due to premier leagues and they are all televised. As soon as a match becomes televised, betting online starts. Compared to many countries, India is the biggest gambling den and maximum numbers of bookies operate here. This has been universally acknowledged. So, we should set an example of creating a regime which includes legislation, specialized groups, investigation bodies, training etc. It seems to be lower down the priority list of the government. If government takes the first step, then the rest will fall into place. It has to start somewhere and someone has to take the first step. What happens in India is that the poor and middle class people lose small amount of money regularly and before they realize they are addicted to gambling."

Legislation abroad

While India is still stuck with its colonial-era laws for legislating gambling in India, other countries like the United Kingdom (UK) and South Africa where sports betting is popular have taken concrete steps to regulate gambling. This section focuses on the legislative measures that have been adopted by both these countries to regulate betting practices.

The Gambling Act was enacted by the UK in 2005 with the following objectives: to prevent gambling from being a source of crime or disorder, to ensure that gambling is conducted in a fair and open way, and to protect children and other vulnerable persons from being harmed or exploited by gambling. The UK Act takes under its ambit any betting practice that includes paying an individual to lose a game deliberately or to profit from a bet placed on the outcome of the game. It also legalizes gambling for adults above the age of eighteen. In order to regulate such betting practices, the Act differentiates between legal and illegal gambling practices to criminalize only certain types of activities. It defines legal betting as making or accepting a bet on the likelihood of anything occurring or not occurring, or of anything being true or not. The outcome of the bet is irrelevant. This broad definition also includes betting on sports. Illegal betting practices include cheating, where a person is prohibited to cheat when gambling or enable or assist another person to cheat. Cheating also consists of actual or attempted deception or interference with the process of gambling or events related to the process of gambling. Thus, spot-fixing and match-fixing (spot-fixing refers to illegal activity in a sport where a specific part of a game is fixed. Something as minor as timing a no ball or wide delivery in cricket is a perfect example of spot-fixing. Whereas match-fixing occurs as a match is played to a completely or partially pre-determined result, violating the rules of the game and often the law), also come under illegal gambling practices because such practices interfere with sports, which would fall under an event related to gambling practices. The UK Act has also kept stringent penalties for committing an offence under the Act. The UK government has also set up a Gambling Commission (www.gamblingcommission.gov.uk), which monitors betting practices to ensure that the Act's objectives are met.

Similarly, betting on sports was banned in South Africa. However, in 2004, the government of South Africa enacted a legislation to regulate betting practices and gambling all over the country, including on sports. The ambit of gambling legislation in South Africa is broad and includes gambling in casinos, betting, wagering, etc. The objective behind the legislation is to promote uniform standards related to gambling practices. Informal bets conducted on a non - commercial basis are also included in the definition of legal gambling and distinguishes between illegal and legal gambling. Only in cases where the outcome of the activity or competition depends on a contingency related to that particular event or is predetermined, betting on such activities is considered to be illegal as it leads to corruption in sports.

A case to legalize gambling in India?

India's Public Gambling Act 1867 does not deter people from gambling. Its provisions are outdated and by criminalizing betting, the Act has only created space for illegal gambling businesses to thrive. Despite the recent incidents of cricketers being found guilty of match-fixing and spot-fixing, betting market in India has remained largely unaffected. As per a Times of India report published in 2010, ahead of the Indian Premier League in 2010, around Rs. 5,000 crore had already been placed on betting per cricket match in India and another two million pounds (over 17 crore Indian rupees) through bookmakers in the UK (Times of India, 2017).

Thus it is apparent that gambling as a recreational activity, especially sports betting is popular among the masses and hence policing this becomes untenable. Currently most legal measures have failed and the law governing gambling is bereft of purpose and is archaic. There is increasing support for the idea that at least some forms of gambling should be legalized but with checks and balances in place. Those who are in support of legalizing gambling view the move to have multiple benefits, including increased revenue generation at the state and central levels, reduction in black money being channeled to fund terror-related and other criminal activities, and a more effective approach to keep a check on the gambling practice in society. Thus it appears necessary to update laws to regulate gambling by providing a legal framework that authorizes betting practices while keeping a check on bookmakers and gambling houses through a strict licensing policy. A good starting point in this regard will be to look at similar laws in other countries and see what can be introduced in India.

Perhaps of greater priority are measures to tackle online gambling. Online betting is becoming very popular in India. Given that existing laws on online betting are lacking and that the IT Act does not cover this, these loopholes are being exploited by offshore betting companies to promote their businesses in India (Hindustan Times, 2017).

Conclusion: the way forward

Gambling as a past time is popular in India. With most forms of gambling deemed illegal, the social and economic ramifications of criminalizing gambling appear to be far-reaching. There is a need to re-visit the archaic laws governing gambling and formulate more appropriate laws. One way to minimize the negative impact of the illegal gambling market in India might be to legalize certain forms of gambling and have stringent measures to regulate it.

Key points

- While opportunities for legal gambling are limited in India, a range of gambling activities continues to be illegal but immensely popular in India.
- The Indian gambling market is estimated to be worth about 60 billion dollars per year, and nearly half the illegal gambling involves betting on cricket. It is estimated that bets worth 200 million dollars are placed on every one-day international match played by the Indian cricket team.
- The illegal gambling market in India has led to the setting up of a parallel economy, which is also funds international crime syndicates involved in drug trafficking and terror-related activities.
- Online gambling is on a steady rise with higher internet penetration, faster connectivity and the smart phone boom. This can lead to a further boom in the already illegal gambling market.
- Gambling laws in India are archaic and although, most legal experts agree that gambling legislation in India is in urgent need of revision there is lack of consensus on what needs to be done.
- A way forward might be to provide a legal framework for gambling in India that authorizes certain betting practices while keeping a check on bookmakers and gambling houses through a strict licensing policy.

References

Ashish, M. (2016). 'Debt due to cricket betting forced Nagpur man into spying' (The Times of India, 2016) http://timesofindia.indiatimes.com/city/jaipur/Debt-due-to-cricket-betting-forced-Nagaur-man-into-spying/articleshow/55236523.cms> accessed 29 September 2017

Benegal, V. (2013). Gambling experiences, problems and policy in India: a historical analysis. *Addiction,* 108, 2062–2067.

Bhide, A. (2007). Compulsive gambling in ancient Indian texts. *Indian Journal of Psychiatry,* 49 (4), 294–295.

K.R. Lakshmanan Vs State Of Tamil Nadu And Anr On 12 January, 1996' (Indiankanoon.org, 2017) <https://indiankanoon.org/doc/1248365/> accessed 6 March 2017.

European Commission 'Study of Gambling Services in the internal market of the European Union' (Swiss institute of Comparative law, 2006) http://ec.europa.eu/internal_market/gambling/docs/study1_en.pdf accessed 29 September 2017

'Gambling Act 2005' (United Kingdom 2005)
'GLOBAL ONLINE GAMBLING AND BETTING MARKET 2015' (www.ystats.com, 2015) <https://www.ystats.com/wp-content/uploads/2015/05/Product-Brochure-Order-Form_Global-Online-Gambling-and-Betting-Market-2015.pdf> accessed 6 March 2017.
'India's Internet Boom' (http://www.deccanchronicle.com/, 2017) <http://www.deccanchronicle.com/opinion/dc-comment/040616/india-s-internet-boom.html> accessed 11 February 2017.
'India Should Legalize Gambling - Times of India' (The Times of India, 2017) <http://timesofindia.indiatimes.com/india/India-should-legalize-gambling/articleshow/5838036.cms> accessed 9 March 2017.
James Thompson, 'Betfair and William Hill target India' (The Independent, 2017) <http://www.independent.co.uk/news/business/news/betfair-and-william-hill-target-india-1810025.html> accessed 8 February 2017.
Ministry of Law, Justice and Company Affairs, 'The Information Technology Act, 2000' (Ministry of Law, Justice and Company Affairs, Government of India 2000)
Ministry of Law and Justice, 'The Public Gambling Act 1867' (Government of India)
Ministry of Law and justice, 'The Constitution of India' (Government of India 2015).
National Crime Records Bureau, 'Crimes in India 2015 Statistics' (Ministry of Home Affairs 2015).
Nirod Kumar Palai, Sarojini Mishra and Kumar Das, 'GAMBLING VS STATE A Study Of Problems And Prospects Of Gambling Industry In India Under Globalization Regime' [2006] XIV International Economic History Congress, Helsinki 2006.
PTI, 'Dawood, Chhota Shakeel behind IPL spot-fixing: Delhi Police' (Livemint, 2013) http://www.livemint.com/Politics/1FyuvH7nwEvHuzmfyVrpsJ/Delhi-Police-invokes-MCOCA-provisions-against-Sreesanth.html accessed 29 September 2017
'Salman Butt And Pakistan Bowlers Jailed For No-Ball Plot - BBC News' (BBC News, 2017) <http://www.bbc.com/news/uk-15573463> accessed 4 March 2017
'SAVING CRICKET: A PROPOSAL FOR THE LEGALIZATION OF GAMBLING IN INDIA TO REGULATE CORRUPT BETTING PRACTICES IN CRICKET' (2017) 26 EMORY INTERNATIONAL LAW REVIEW <http://file:///C:/Users/Smriti%20Singh/Desktop/gambling%20chapter/reading%203pdf.pdf> accessed 9 February 2017.
Sruthin Lal, 'With $200 Million on every ODI match, Illegal betting thrives in India' (http://www.hindustantimes.com/, 2017) <http://www.hindustantimes.com/business/with-200-million-on-every-odi-match-illegal-betting-thrives/story-5CDuIIgCrykqM2smIPn7dI.html> accessed 10 March 2017.
'The Cronje Chronicles' (Cricinfo, 2017) <http://www.espncricinfo.com/ci/content/story/654219.html> accessed 7 February 2017.
'The Pakistan Spot-Fixing Case | In Focus | Cricket News | ESPN Cricinfo' (Cricinfo, 2017) <http://www.espncricinfo.com/infocus/content/story/infocus.html?subject=44> accessed 1 March 2017.
Somshuvra Laha, 'Legally Illegal, But You Can Bet Online In India' (http://www.hindustantimes.com/, 2017) <http://www.hindustantimes.com/india/legally-illegal-but-you-can-bet-online-in-india/story-SW04haVrqOq1MzlFBvOjiP.html> accessed 15 February 2017.

Chapter 5

Gambling research from India

Sanju George

Introduction

The field of gambling/gambling disorder has not been subject to much systematic research in India.

There have only been three published research studies on gambling from India. These three will be discussed below. There have also been 2 other non-research papers published on gambling from India: the first was a short review of 'Compulsive gambling in ancient Indian texts' by Dr Bhide (2007) published in the Indian Journal of Psychiatry, and the second was a narrative review titled 'Gambling experiences, problems and policy in India: a historical analysis' by Dr Benegal, published in 2013 in the journal Addiction. I will also briefly mention some findings from an ongoing study (personal communication). All other writing on gambling-related topics from India have been non-academic – i.e. in newspapers and lay publications.

1. **'Gambling addiction in India: Should psychiatrists care?'** (George et al, 2014)

This was a survey of psychiatrists' 'exposure' to gamblers in their practice, their attitudes towards gamblers, their views on the 'place' of gambling addiction within psychiatry, their awareness and knowledge of problem gambling, etc. 121 psychiatrists working in various parts of India, who had come to attend a national psychiatric conference participated in the survey and completed questionnaires. The questionnaire consisted of some demographic questions, some questions which could be given yes/no answers, some statements with the option of choosing the following responses: strongly agree, agree, neither agree nor disagree, disagree and strongly disagree, and two open-ended questions. Statements to which psychiatrists could give one of these five responses (strongly agree, agree, neither agree nor disagree, disagree and strongly disagree) included: exposure to patients with gambling addiction, teaching/training in the management of gambling addiction, understanding of gambling addiction, perception of your roles in management of gambling addicts and their views on its feasibility, and so on.

This study showed that 80.9% of psychiatrists had seen patients with gambling addiction in their clinical practice. However only 19.1% reported ever having received any teaching or training in the management of gambling addicts. This is a significant gap in current psychiatric training. More encouragingly, 90.2% of psychiatrists said it was feasible for them to be involved in the treatment of gambling addicts, and 80.7% of those said they would like to receive further training in this area. Equally encouraging was the proportion that viewed gambling as a public health problem (89.1%) and those who saw it as an addictive disorder (93.6%).

2. **A cross-sectional study of problem gambling and its correlates among college students in South India** (George et al, 2016).

This study evaluated the prevalence of gambling participation and problem gambling among college students in India, and also looked at demographic and psychosocial correlates of gambling in that sample. 5784 college students from 58 colleges in Kerala, India were selected for the study using cluster random sampling. The questionnaires addressed gambling, substance use, psychological distress, suicidality and attention-deficit hyperactivity disorder (ADHD).

5580 completed questionnaires were analysed. The mean age of the sample was 19.5 years (range=17–25 years). 1917 respondents were men (34.4%) and 3663 (65.6%) women. 1090/5580 (19.5%) individuals had gambled at least once and of these 675 (12.1%) were non-problem gamblers and 415 (7.4%) were problem gamblers. Of the 1090 individuals who had ever gambled, 415 (38.1%) were problem gamblers.

In terms of participation in various forms of gambling activities, lottery was the most popular form of gambling, followed by betting on football and cricket, and playing card games. Only a small minority reported gambling online; 787 (14.1%) had participated in only one type of gambling activity, 195 (4.3%) had participated in two forms of gambling, 66 (1.0%) had participated in three forms of gambling and 42 (0.6%) students had taken part in more than three types.

Problem gamblers when compared with non-gamblers were significantly more likely to be male, have a part-time job, have poor academic performance, higher lifetime use of alcohol, tobacco and cannabis, greater psychological distress, more suicidal thoughts and attempts, and higher ADHD symptom scores .

In summary, only 19.5% of college students in this study reported having ever gambled. This is considerably lower than that found in previous studies from Asia in young people where gambling participation rate has varied between 32 and 60%. Authors offered the following possible explanations for this crucial finding: due to the limited availability of gambling; a lack of acceptance of gambling as a leisure activity in the Indian culture; the questionnaires used may not have reliably and validly assessed gambling in Indian students; or perhaps Indian students are less willing to admit to gambling than those in other countries. Yet another key finding authors of this study highlight is that of the people who ever gambled, more than one-third (38.1%) was classified as problem gamblers. Thus, although the rate of gambling was low in comparison to studies from other countries, the overall prevalence of problem gambling was 7.4%, within the range of that reported in other college student samples. These data suggest that in India, there are significantly high rates of problem gambling among those who gamble. This could mean that a higher proportion of students who gamble are likely to develop problems from it.

3. **Do high school students in India gamble? A study of problem gambling and its correlates** (Jaisoorya et al, 2017).

This study explored the point prevalence of gambling and its psychosocial correlates among high school students in Kerala, India. Methodologically this study was similar to the earlier – described study of gambling among college students, as these were carried out by the same research group.

This was a single stage, cross - sectional epidemiological survey carried out in single random classes of years 10 and 12 in 73 schools selected by cluster random sampling from the total pool of 168 high and higher secondary schools in the district of Ernakulam, Kerala.

The questionnaires were self-completed, pencil and paper type and were administered in a class room setting. Apart from gambling, other domains assessed included the use of alcohol and tobacco, psychological distress, suicidality, symptoms of attention deficit hyperactivity disorder and exposure to childhood sexual abuse. Of the questionnaires returned, 4989 questionnaires were included in the analyses. The mean age of the sample was 16.3±1.03 years (range = 15 to 19 years) and 2510 (50.8%) were boys.

Of the total sample, 1400 (27.9%) individuals had gambled at least once. 1047 (20.8%) were classified as non-problem gamblers and 353 (7.1%) as problem gamblers. Of those who had ever gambled, 25.2% were problem gamblers. The most popular forms of gambling were betting on football and cricket followed by playing the lottery and festival gambling. Among those who gambled, 814 (58.1%) had only participated in one type of gambling activity, 271 (19.4%) had participated in two gambling activities, 101 (2.0%) had participated in three types of gambling activities, and 42 (0.6%) students had taken part in more than three types of gambling activities.

Male sex and part time job were significantly higher in the problem gambling group as compared to the non-problem gambling and non-gambling groups. The highest rates of academic failures, substance use, psychological distress, suicidality, sexual abuse and ADHD scores were in the problem gambling group, followed by non-problem gambling group and the non-gambling group.

So in summary, only 27.5% of this sample reported having ever gambled which is much lower than that found in other studies of young people in other parts of the world. 7.1% of the sample were identified as problem gamblers. Perhaps most importantly, of those students who ever gambled, a quarter (25.2%)\ were classified as problem gamblers suggesting that in India there are significantly high rates of problem gambling among those who gamble.

Authors end on a cautionary note by stating that gambling among high school students is clearly associated with psychological problems and that the increased availability of and accessibility to gambling opportunities in India, especially remote gambling (online and phone) will likely lead to an increase in both rates of gambling participation and problem gambling in young people.

4. Benegal et al (personal communication) looked at the prevalence of gambling and problem gambling (as measured by the Canadian Problem Gambling Index) in three patient samples (treatment seekers, internet responders and controls) and found the following rates of gambling and problem gambling respectively - treatment seekers = 13% and 7.4%; controls = 4.5% and 0%; internet responders = 19.6% and 0%). They also noted that card games involving money were the most popular form of gambling activity.

Funding gambling research

This is an issue which warrants further debate. Should research funding come from the gambling industry or from other non-gambling related/ 'independent' sources? Ethically the most robust model should avoid any funding from the gambling industry. Purists see such money as 'blood money'. If funding from the gambling industry is rejected, then one is exclusively dependent on the government or other 'independent' sources for funding. Or one could be more pragmatic and take the position that funding from the industry can be accepted but on the condition that it is subject to strict ethical scrutiny and that an ethical code of practice will be in place and closely monitored.

For robust research to be conducted, adequate funding is a pre-requisite. And for that, traditional medical and social research funding bodies need to be on board. A greater degree of public awareness of gambling as a potential problem, and mental health care professionals and their respective professional bodies framing it as a public health issue will both help calls for greater research funding.

Recommendations for future research

It is only reasonable to say that gambling disorder/addiction has historically been neglected and continues to be the 'poor step child' of addiction psychiatry. Further studies need to be carried out to estimate the prevalence of gambling and gambling disorder among the general population in India. In addition gambling habits of high-risk groups such as young people, and those with comorbid mental disorders or other addictions, need further exploration. There should also be studies looking at the effectiveness of various treatment interventions, course and prognosis, etc. For relevant research to be carried out, adequate and appropriate funding is essential:

Key points

- The area of gambling/gambling disorder has not been subjected to systematic research in India as evidenced by only three published research studies on gambling from India.
- A study of psychiatrists working in India found that although more than three - quarters of psychiatrists had seen patients with gambling addiction in their clinical practice only 19% had ever received any teaching or training in the treatment of these patients. However, 90% of psychiatrists viewed gambling as a public health problem and said it was feasible for them to be involved in the treatment of gambling addicts.
- Two methodologically similar cross-sectional studies looked at the prevalence of problem gambling and its correlates among school and college students respectively. Lottery was

the most popular form of gambling in both these groups and problem gamblers when compared with non-gamblers were significantly more likely to be male, have poor academic performance, higher lifetime use of alcohol, tobacco and cannabis, greater psychological distress, more suicidal thoughts and attempts, and higher ADHD symptom scores. Although only a quarter of these samples had ever gambled, more than one-third of these were classified as problem gamblers.

- Further research is warranted and for robust research to be conducted, adequate funding is a pre-requisite. Ideally, research funding should be sourced from non-gambling related/ 'independent' sources and not from the gambling industry, this would be ethically most robust. However one could also be more pragmatic: in a world with scarce funding opportunities, funding from the industry can be accepted but on the condition that it is subject to strict ethical scrutiny, monitoring and regulation.

References

Benegal, V. (2013). Gambling experiences, problems and policy in India: a historical analysis. *Addiction* 108, 2062–2067.

Bhide, A. (2007). Compulsive gambling in ancient Indian texts. *Indian Journal of Psychiatry*, 49 (4), 294–295.

George, S., Kallivayalil, R., Jaisoorya, T. S. (2014). Gambling addiction in India: Should psychiatrists care? *Indian Journal of Psychiatry*, 56 (2): 111-112.

George, S., Jaisoorya, T.S., Sivasankaran, N.B., Rani, A., Menon, P., Madhavan, R. et al. (2016). A cross-sectional study of problem gambling and its correlates among college students in South India. *British Journal of Psychiatry Open*, *2*(3):199- 203.

Jaisoorya, T. S., Beena, K. V., Beena, M., Ellangovan, K., Thennarassu, K., Bowden-Jones, H. (2017). Do High School Students in India Gamble? A Study of Problem Gambling and Its Correlates. Journal of Gambling Studies. 33(2):449-460

Chapter 6

Gambling – A public health perspective in the Indian context

Lokesh Shekhawat and Jaisoorya TS

Introduction

Gambling is defined as any activity which includes putting something at risk to gain money or property and where gain is uncertain and determined by chance. Gambling across the world is a common form of entertainment and has existed in some form for thousands of years. In India it has deep roots as a common form of recreation in the tradition and culture of society. The oldest description of gambling in the world can be traced to the Rig Veda and Atharva Veda, two ancient Indian scriptures (Bhide, 2007). Gambling is also the cornerstone of the oldest Indian mythological text, the Mahabharata, which is essentially the tale of a righteous King Yudhishtira gambling to lose his kingdom, his brothers and himself, and in his desperation to win, stakes his wife Draupadi and loses her, leading to humiliation and war (Bhide, 2007).

While for most people gambling remains a leisure activity, for some, it can become problematic. Gambling exists on a spectrum or continuum of escalating severity from recreational activity to problematic behaviour to addiction with increasing severity being associated with more adverse consequences. Gambling becomes problematic when it begins to disrupt or damage personal, family or recreational pursuits (Lesieur and Rosenthal, 1991). At the most severe end of the spectrum is gambling disorder which refers to a condition related to excessive gambling and defined by criteria set forth in the Diagnostic and Statistical Manual of Mental Disorder 5 (DSM-5) (APA, 2013). Patients with gambling disorder need to meet at least four of the nine diagnostic criteria which include the need to gamble with increasing amounts of money in order to achieve the desired excitement; restless or irritable when attempting to cut down or stop gambling; has made repeated unsuccessful efforts to control, cut back, or stop gambling; is often preoccupied with gambling, gambling while distressed; "chasing" one's losses; lying regarding extent of gambling; personal, social, occupational disruption; and needs financial support to overcome financial crisis necessitated by gambling.

The current legal framework of gambling in India

Despite the popular tradition and culture of gambling in India, the Public Gambling Act 1867, (http://www.sangrurpolice.in/wpcontent/themes/intrepidity/images/actrule/publicGamblingAct1867.pdf) the only law that regulates gambling, prohibits any game based on chance or probability. Thus games of pure chance such as satta are illegal and games of skill and not just mere chance such as horse racing are legal. After independence, through List II of the seventh schedule of the constitution, the centre has devolved exclusive powers to individual states to deem what types of gambling are legal or illegal within their state boundaries. Currently, lotteries are legal in 13 of the 29 Indian states and 5 Union territories, horse racing is legal only in six states and casinos are legal only in two states (Goa and Sikkim). Online gambling comes under the Information Technology Act 2000, (http://deity.gov.in/content/view-it-act-2000), which makes all forms of online gambling illegal.

Does gambling in India merit a public health approach?

Given that gambling in most forms is illegal, it is to be expected that gambling rates and participation in India are low. But this appears not to be the case, as there are anecdotal reports of illegal, organised gambling syndicates for betting on cricket, with an estimated Rs.30,000 crore [nearly $4.4 billion] having been bet on the 2016 T 20 Cricket World Cup (Economic Times, 2016).Accurate figures on the amount of money spent on gambling across the country are lacking, but estimates from 1997 suggest that India's gambling market was worth approximately $60 billion dollars per year, of which about half was illegal, which amounts to around 3.5% of India's Gross Domestic Product (KPMG). There are no published studies on prevalence of gambling among adults in India. Two recent surveys of school and college students in the state of Kerala reported problem gambling rates of 7.1% and 7.4% respectively (Jaisoorya et al, 2017; George et al, 2016). World - over the prevalence of recreational gambling is reported to vary between 10 and 70% with the difference mostly accounted for by the variance in acceptance of gambling across cultures. Pathological form of gambling is a major public health issue in high-income countries with past–year problem gambling rates reported to range from 0.12 to 5.8% and gambling disorder rates reported to range from 0.4 to 1.0% across different countries in the world (Calado & Griffiths, 2016).

The current concept of public health is not limited to disease control and prevention but also concerns overall promotion of health of the population. It targets the organized efforts of all sections of society to deal with all components of health and to extend health promotion from the individual to the entire society. In India, public health has made only slow progress owing to low expenditure on health (Chauhan, 2011). Indian public health priorities currently remain control of infections, sanitation, and maternal and infant health. Mental health funding remain abysmally low with the priority being to ensure community treatment for people with severe mental illness. It is against this background that an attempt is made to examine whether there is a case for gambling disorder meriting a public health response in India.

1. ***Gambling's harm to the individual:*** The most concrete form of harm from gambling to the individual is financial harm, with most reporting large debts, poverty and even bankruptcy. Problem gamblers also have significant disruption, conflict, breakdown and estrangement in relationships (Velleman et al, 2015). Gamblers are less productive at work and often involve in criminal activities relating to fraud and embezzlement to address financial demands of gambling (Victorian Competition and Efficiency Commission, 2012). In addition, harms which are often not apparent include higher rates of psychosomatic illness/symptoms (cardiovascular, gastrointestinal, etc.) (Morasco et al, 2006) and psychiatric illnesses like anxiety, depression, substance use, suicidality and personality disorders (Petry et al, 2005) experienced by problem gamblers.
2. ***The social harms of gambling:*** Problematic levels of gambling can have adverse consequences on the family and the community. For each problem gambler, there are approximately five to seven people negatively impacted. There is increased family disruption, lowered work productivity, increased level of criminal activities, financial disruption following debt and bankruptcy, perpetuation of poverty, increased reliance on social and health services, and disruption of social cohesion (Langham et al, 2016).

3. ***Gambling impacts the most vulnerable:*** Higher rates of gambling are reported in adolescents and among those in the lowest socio-economic strata of society. A meta-analysis found that there is a 13% life time prevalence for problem gambling and pathological gambling among adolescents (Shaffer et al, 1999). Further, studies have shown that those who begin to gamble at an earlier age have a higher risk of developing persistence and two to three times higher risk of problem gambling and pathological gambling in youth (Derevensky & Gupta, 2000). Studies have also shown that subjects from lower socio-economic status are more vulnerable to the financial harms of gambling. Greater social acceptance and the media can influence gambling both among adolescents and subjects from lower socio-economic status.

4. ***Targeted interventions for gambling:*** Targeted efforts may have benefits as recent studies have identified risk factors for gambling. Johansson et al (2008) carried out a review and reported risk factors which the authors defined as 'well-established' and 'probable': They found that younger age, male gender, delinquency, involvement in illegal acts, alcohol and other drug problems, and obsessive-compulsive disorder are well-established resk factor and unemployment, lower socio-economic status, living in a large urban centre, lower academic achievement, impulsivity, poor coping styles and sensation seeking, depression, anxiety, and personality disorders are probable risk factors for gambling.

5. ***Accessibility to gambling and prevalence:*** Blaszczynski & Nower's (2002) biopsychosocial model suggests that accessibility to gambling is an integral component in the development of problem gambling. This hypothesis has been tested and studies have found that increased availability (Ladouceur et al, 2005) and accessibility (Sevigny et al, 2008) of gambling increases involvement in gambling which further increases prevalence of gambling disorders. Though gambling activities are legally restricted in India, with increasing technology penetrance, easy availability of the internet and gambling apps there is likely to be a spurt in gambling participation and problem gambling.

6. ***Is the gambling scenario in India concerning?***

   Gambling in India remains understudied. The major constraint in gambling research in India is that most forms of gambling remain illegal hence preventing disclosure, despite its popularity. There have been no Indian studies on gambling in adults. But two studies in school and college students from the state of Kerala reported some disconcerting findings (George et al, 2016; Jaisoorya et al, 2016). Students reported participating in a wide variety of gambling activities of which the most common was betting on cricket but many others reported participating in festival card games, betting on animal fights, sophisticated card games like poker, lottery, internet gambling, betting on horse racing and other sports, etc. Although the prevalence of gambling was low, the proportion of subjects who had problem gambling among those who gambled was significantly higher in comparison to studies from high income countries. Furthermore, subjects with problem gambling in both these studies from India had numerous negative correlates such as greater academic failures, higher substance use, higher psychological distress scores and higher suicidality, similar to correlates reported from studies in high income countries among young people (Hyder et al, 2008). Thus these findings suggest that negative correlates of problematic gambling remain cross-culturally similar. Further, with increasing technological penetrance in India, the expected availability of and accessibility to gambling opportunities will most likely lead to a spurt in all forms of gambling.

Thus, to summarize, harms reported from problematic gambling are varied and diffuse, unlike the more direct and visible harms caused by physical illnesses or substance addictions. A range of harms that adversely affects the individual, the family and society have been reported. Although most gambling activities in India are illegal, anecdotal reports suggest that gambling is immensely popular with substantial amounts being spent on gambling activities. With increasing westernisation and technological penetration in India, it is expected that problems related to gambling are likely to increase. It is against this background that it is pertinent to conceptualise an appropriate public health response to gambling in India.

There are no published studies or known research projects in India on public health responses to gambling. Most published work are from high income countries where gambling is recognised as a major public health problem. Thus this conceptualisation of a public health response to gambling in India is a summary of the public health responses with the best evidence from across the world with suggested modifications relevant to the Indian context.

Importance of prevention

High priority needs to be given to preventive approaches to tackle the public health challenges posed by gambling. Preventive efforts have proven effectiveness and have effectively lowered the rates of individuals requiring treatment for mental health issues (National Research Council, 1999). Preventive approaches would be of greater benefit if they targets the most vulnerable, which in the case of gambling includes young people. The other important group vulnerable to greater harm in the Indian context is those individuals with low income. The most often talked about primary preventive strategy is the risk and protective factors model.

Risk and protective factors model

There are very few primary preventive strategies whose effectiveness have been tested in gambling. One model, the risk and protective factors model, has been widely used in tackling addictions among youth (Bournstein et al, 1999) and has been applied to problem gambling prevention (Dickson et al, 2002).

This model aims to understand the initiation of health-protective behaviours and health-risk behaviours such as gambling, as well as the potential to modify these problem behaviours. Programs based on this model seek to eliminate or minimize risk factors associated with specific negative outcomes and enhance factors that predict positive outcomes.

While children with specific risk factors, like those whose parents/ siblings have issues of gambling or addiction, more so when there is an earlier age of onset and positive attitudes towards gambling it may be heuristically attractive to tailor specific programs. But broadly, it appears that certain risk factors for gambling are shared across adolescent problem behaviours (e.g. impulsivity, poor parental supervision, and deviant friends). Hence a cost - effective and practical conceptual approach would be to target these shared problems during adolescence rather than developing prevention programs for isolated problem behaviours.

Levels of prevention framework

The framework which has the widest application in public health across both mental and physical illnesses is the concept of levels of prevention. The levels of prevention concept aims to comprehensively respond to public health issues with a three tier response. Traditionally these initiatives have been categorized into the three levels: primary (or 'universal'), secondary (or 'indicated'), and tertiary prevention (or 'selective') each with specific health goals (Caplan, 1964).

One of the comprehensive approaches attempted based on the above model in the area of gambling is that promoted by Independent Pricing and Regulatory Tribunal (IPART) of New South Wales Australia, which promotes a policy of responsible gambling (IPART, 2004).

As per the framework, the broad goals of primary prevention would be to focus on preventing or postponing initiation into the first bet. Secondary prevention aims at screening for potential problems for those who are initiated and tertiary prevention aims preventing further harm in those who already exhibit problematic levels of gambling (e.g. specialised treatment for problem gamblers).

Primary prevention

Primary prevention takes a universal approach and targets gamblers and non-gamblers. Primary prevention is more effective when a multimodal approach is used encompassing culturally - sensitive social, psychological and legal strategies. Broadly, primary preventive approaches followed across the world aim to make the general public aware of the risks and potential negative consequences of excessive gambling, and help them make decisions about 'responsible' gambling. The information provided must include general information about gambling (awareness of risks associated with gambling, awareness of how gambling products work and the probability of winning). It should also encourage individuals to take responsibility for their gambling, recognise early warning signs of problem gambling in oneself and others, and promote awareness of the availability of appropriate help. It will be feasible and cost effective in the Indian context if these campaigns are integrated into existing school and college-based intervention measures/ programmes for substance addictions and other mental health issues. Furthermore, these campaigns may be timed to target certain sporting events such as cricket tournaments which are known to lead to "gambling spikes" in the community.

Regulation of advertisements and promotions of gambling is another commonly employed strategy. Both direct and surrogate advertising for gambling is banned in India expect for state - sponsored lotteries. But most advertising especially targeting young people is through the social media which has little monitoring and often beyond the control of regulatory agencies. It is thus necessary in India to ensure enforcement of regulations in all forms of media. Further, the use of gambling revenue to fund social programs, mostly lotteries, in India has created a social distinction between good and bad gambling (involving other forms like card games, casinos, etc.) which needs to be addressed.

Secondary prevention

Secondary prevention measures involve two aspects, both of which aim to target 'at risk' and problem gamblers. The first aspect aims to ensure early diagnosis and treatment for the individual. The vast majority of (>90%) of individuals with gambling - related disorders do not seek formal treatment. Denial, shame and wanting to handle the problem themselves are the most frequently perceived reasons for barriers in treatment seeking. Lack of knowledge about the disorder and available treatment options have also been cited as significant barriers (Suurvali et al, 2009). Further, most of these individuals' presentations to healthcare agencies are non-gambling related or 'indirect', such as physical/medical symptoms, and/or psychiatric symptoms (depression, anxiety, substance misuse, etc.). A combination of these factors coupled with lack of training for and competence of health care professionals to deal with gambling–related problems result in problem gamblers often going undiagnosed and untreated.

The second aspect involves the gaming industry's self-regulation to ensure reduced harm to their clients. Some such steps proposed include gaming staff undergoing training to identify at risk gamblers; self-exclusion programs for problem gamblers; modifications to player environments and gaming machines designed to protect against impulsive decision making and excessive play (e.g. removal of ATMs from gaming areas, restricted areas for accessing cash, etc.); and improved access and awareness of helpline and treatment services through signage and other printed material in gaming centres.

Tertiary prevention

Tertiary prevention strategies involve specialized interventions targeting individuals experiencing harm from their own gambling or through their loved one's gambling. A range of treatment options have been tried. Psychological treatments are the mainstay of treatment and cognitive behaviour therapy (CBT) has the best evidence base. CBT targets the gambler's cognitive distortions (overestimating probabilities of winning, illusions of control over the outcome of a bet, the belief that a win is due after a series of losses and memory biases in favour of remembering wins (Toneatto, 1999). At the severe end of the spectrum, those with gambling disorder require pharmacological and psychological treatments as well as addressing the secondary issues caused by gambling. Brief telephone - based motivational interviewing treatment combined with e - mailed self-help cognitive-behavioural therapy workbook have found to be effective in people with gambling disorders who were not willing to seek help (Hodgins et al, 2009).

A group intervention modelled on the Alcoholics Anonymous, Gamblers Anonymous, is also very popular, although treatment studies have shown poor attendance and outcome (Hodgins et al, 2011). Gamblers Anonymous also runs support groups for families and friends called Gam-Anon.

In India, there are no specialised treatment centres for gambling. Given the constraints in financial and human resources in mental health, it is suggested that treatment services ought to be integrated into existing addiction or mental health service delivery structures, rather than being stand-alone gambling treatment centres. Further a tiered model for delivery of treatment services for problem gamblers (George & Copello, 2011), ranging from non - specialist/generic services that provide information, screening and onward referral, to specialist services that offer brief interventions, CBT, pharmacotherapy, in-patient care and rehabilitation services may be offered. Such an approach will ensure cost effectiveness and sustainability.

Role of families

Culturally in India, families have played a significant role in providing support and one of the important reasons cited for good outcome of severe mental illnesses in India is the positive role played by the family. There is evidence that even though families are disrupted by gambling, involvement of family members in treatment improves both outcome, and individual and family functioning (Ingle et al, 2008). Hence, potentially, family members can function as first contacts to identify early signs of gambling disorder, and involving and empowering them in treatment interventions can not only be cost effective but also help in improving outcomes.

Future directions

Gambling in India is understudied and the priority would be to address the lack of quality research to understand the extent of gambling and related harm. Any such research should ideally be multi - sectorial, involving health, finance, legal and social frameworks. Second, there is an urgent need to sensitize the public, educators, healthcare professionals, policymakers and other stake holders on the challenges posed by gambling and the likelihood of gambling activities increasing in the future. Third is to address skill deficits among medical professionals by providing specialized training to ensure early recognition and treatment of gambling disorder. Lastly, gambling laws in India are archaic and need reform. While reform of gambling laws may require a wider debate and weighing up evidence - based policies, the alternative would be to ban certain types of gambling while legalising certain gambling venues which are tightly regulated and taxed.

Conclusion

Gambling is ingrained in Indian culture and tradition. Though most forms of gambling are currently deemed unlawful in India, it remains immensely popular. Preliminary work from India suggests that people reporting problem gambling have numerous negative correlates. It is thus important to formulate an appropriate public health response. A comprehensive approach of improving awareness, facilitating research, preventive strategies targeting the most vulnerable, ensuring early recognition and treatment of those affected, alongside debating the need for appropriate reform of the current legal framework is the best way forward.

Key points

- The current concept of public health is not limited to disease control and prevention but also concerns overall promotion of health of the population.
- Gambling disorder merits a public health response in India because: it is a significant problem in terms of its prevalence, harms caused to the individual, family and society, its impact on the most vulnerable, and its increasing accessibility.
- An effective framework for a public health response to gambling in India is the levels of prevention. The levels of prevention model aims to comprehensively respond to public health issues with a three - tiered response categorized into the three levels: primary (or 'universal'), secondary (or 'indicated'), and tertiary prevention (or 'selective') each with specific health goals.

References

American Psychiatric Association. (2013). Diagnostic and Statistical Manual of Mental Disorders (5th edn) (DSM-5). APA.

Bhide, A. V. (2007). Compulsive gambling in ancient Indian texts. *Indian Journal of Psychiatry*, 49:294-5.

Blaszczynski, A. & Nower, L. (2002). A pathways model of problem and pathological gambling. *Addiction*, 97, 487–499.

Bournstein, P. J., Zweig, J. M., Gardner, S. E. (1999). Understanding substance abuse prevention: Toward the 21st century: A primer on effective programs. Rockville, MD: Department of Health and Human Services, Substance Abuse and Mental Health Services Administration, Center for Substance Abuse Prevention, Division of Knowledge Development and Evaluation.

Calado, F. & Griffiths, M. D. (2016). Problem gambling worldwide: An update and systematic review of empirical research (2000-2015). *Journal of Behavioural Addictions*, 5:592-613.
Caplan, G. (1964). Principles of preventive psychiatry. Basic Books, New York.
Independent Pricing, Regulatory Tribunal. Gambling: Promoting a culture of responsibility. Sydney: Independent Pricing and Regulatory Tribunal of New South Wales; 2004.
Chauhan, L. S. (2011). Public health in India: Issues and Challenges. *Indian Journal of Public Health*, 55:88-91.
Derevensky, J. L. & Gupta. R. (2000). Prevalence estimates of adolescent gambling: a comparison of the SOGS-RA, DSM-IV-J, and the GA 20 Questions. *Journal of Gambling Studies*, 16, 289-313.
Dickson, L., Derevensky, J., Gupta, R. (2002). The prevention of youth gambling problems: A conceptual model. *Journal of Gambling Studies*, 18, 97–159.
George, S. & Copello, A. (2011). Treatment provision for Britain's problem gamblers: present gaps and future opportunities. *Advances in Psychiatric Treatment*, 17: 318-22.
George, S., Jaisoorya, T. S., Nair, S., Rani, A., Menon, P., Madhavan, R. et al. (2016). A cross-sectional study of problem gambling and its correlates among college students in South India. *British Journal of Psychiatry Open*, 199- 203.
Hodgins, D. C., Stea, J. N., Grant, J. E. (2011). Gambling disorders. *The Lancet*. 378:1874-84.
Petry, N. M., Ammerman, Y., Bohl, J., Doersch, A., Gay, H., Kadden, R. et al. (2006). Cognitive-behavioural therapy for pathological gamblers. *Journal of Consulting and Clinical Psychology*, 74: 555–67.
IT Act. (2000). http://deity.gov.in/content/view-it-act-2000. (Accessed on 2 January 2018).
http://economictimes.indiatimes.com/news/sports/indias-world-t20-semifinals-loss-crores-of-rupees-were-lost-in-betting/articleshow/51655707.cms. (Accessed on 30 September 2017).
Hyder, A. A. & Juul, N. H. (2008). Games, gambling, and children: Applying the precautionary principle for child health. Journal of Child and Adolescent Psychiatric Nursing, 21(4), 202-204.
Ingle, P. J., Marotta, J., McMillan, G. (2008). Significant others and gambling treatment outcomes. *Journal of Gambling Studies*, 24(3):381-92.
Jaisoorya, T. S., Beena, K. V., Beena, M., Ellangovan, K., Thennarassu, K., Bowden-Jones, H. et al. (2016). Do high school students in India gamble? A study of problem gambling and its correlates. *Journal of Gambling Studies*, 1-12.
Johansson, A., Grant, J. E., Kim, S. W., Odlaug, B. L., Gotestam, K. G. (2008). Risk factors for problematic gambling: a critical literature review. *Journal of Gambling Studies*, 25, 67–92.
Ladouceur, R., Jacques, C., Sevigny, E., Cantinotti, M. (2005). Impact of the format, arrangement, and availability of electronic gaming machines outside casinos on gambling. *International Gambling Studies*, 5, 139–154.
Langham, E., Thorne, H., Browne, M., Donaldson, P., Rose, J., Rocklof, M. et al. (2016). Understanding gambling related harm: a proposed definition, conceptual framework, and taxonomy of harms. *BMC Public Health*, 16:80.
Lesieur, H. R. & Rosenthal, R. J. (1991). Pathological gambling: a review of literature (prepared for the American Psychiatric Association Task Force of DSM-IV committee on Disorders of Impulse Control Not Elsewhere Classified). *Journal of Gambling Studies*, 7, 5-39.

Morasco, B. J., Pietrzak, R. H., Blanco, C., Grant, B. F., Hasin, D., Petry, N. M. (2006). Health problems and medical utilization associated with gambling disorders: results from the National Epidemiologic Survey on alcohol and related conditions. *Psychosomatics*, 68, 976–984.

National Research Council. (1999). Pathological gambling: A critical review. Washington, DC: National Academy Press.

Petry, N. M., Stinson, F. S., Grant, B. F. (2005). Comorbidity of DSM-IV pathological gambling and other psychiatric disorders: results from the National Epidemiologic Survey on Alcohol and Related Conditions. *Journal of Clinical Psychiatry*, 66, 564–574.

Sevigny, S., Ladouceur, R., Jacques, C., Cantinotti, M. (2008). Links between casino proximity and gambling participation, expenditure, and pathology. Psychology of *Addictive Behaviours*, 22, 295–301.

Shaffer, H. J., Hall, M. N., Vander Bilt, J. (1999). Estimating the prevalence of disordered gambling behaviour in the United States and Canada: A research synthesis. *American Journal of Public Health*, 89(9):1369-76.

Summerfield, M. & Loo, W. (2010). Online Gaming: A Gamble or a Sure Bet? KPMG International.

Suurvali, H., Cordingley, J., Hodgins, D. C., Cunningham, J. (2009). Barriers to seeking help for gambling problems: A review of the empirical literature. *Journal of Gambling Studies*, 25:407–424.

Toneatto, T. (1999). Cognitive psychopathology of problem gambling. *Substance Use and Misuse*, *34*: 1593–604.

Velleman, R., Cousins, J., Orford, J. (2015). The effects of gambling on the family. In: H. Bowden-Jones, S. George (Eds.) *A Clinician's Guide to Working with Problem Gamblers*. Routledge, London.

Victorian Competition and Efficiency Commission (2012). Counting the cost: Inquiry into the costs of problem gambling. Draft report. Melbourne: Victorian Competition and Efficiency Commission.

Welte, J., Barnes, G., Wieczorek, W., Tidwell, M., Parker. (2001). Alcohol and gambling pathology among U.S. adults: prevalence, demographic patterns and comorbidity. *Journal of Studies on Alcohol and Drugs*, 62(5), 706–712.

Chapter 7

Gambling disorder: Screening and assessment

Jayant Mahadevan and Arun Kandasamy

Introduction

Gambling disorder has been a part of psychiatric nosology for more than three decades. It was first introduced as a mental disorder in the Diagnostic and Statistical Manual of mental disorders (DSM III) and was called 'pathological gambling', a term which has since been deemed pejorative and stigmatizing. Gambling disorder has thus far been classified under the rubric of impulse control disorders until the DSM – 5 (APA, 2013) where owing to mounting evidence, it has been conceptualized as an addictive disorder. Diagnostic criteria for the same are listed in Table.1 and mirror those of other substance addictions.

Table. 7.1. DSM – 5 criteria for gambling disorder
Persistent and recurrent problematic gambling behaviour leading to clinically significant impairment or distress, as indicated by the individual exhibiting four (or more) of the following in a 12-month period:
1. Needs to gamble with increasing amounts of money in order to achieve the desired excitement.
2. Is restless or irritable when attempting to cut down or stop gambling.
3. Has made repeated unsuccessful efforts to control, cut back, or stop gambling.
4. Is often preoccupied with gambling (e.g. having persistent thoughts of reliving past gambling experiences, handicapping or planning the next venture, thinking of ways to get money with which to gamble).
5. Often gambles when feeling distressed (e.g. helpless, guilty, anxious, depressed).

6. After losing money gambling, often returns another day to get even ("chasing" one's losses).
7. Lies to conceal the extent of involvement with gambling.
8. Has jeopardized or lost a significant relationship, job, or educational or career opportunity because of gambling.
9. Relies on others to provide money to relieve desperate financial situations caused by gambling.

The gambling behaviour is not better accounted for by a manic episode Current severity:

Mild: 4–5 criteria met, Moderate: 6–7 criteria met, Severe: 8–9 criteria met.

Internationally, epidemiological studies estimate that the prevalence of past-year adult pathological gambling to be between 1.1 and 3.5% (Shaffer et al, 1999; Shaffer and Hall, 2001; Welte et al, 2002). Recent research also estimates that 6 to 9 percent of young people and young adults experience problems related to gambling — a higher rate than among adults (Barnes et al, 2010). This underlines the fact that gambling disorder is a common condition. It however remains under-recognized in clinical practice. In the Indian context, accounts of different forms of gambling find mention in culture right from ancient times.

A shift in the nosological position of gambling disorder in DSM - 5, changes to the diagnostic criteria and changes in the diagnostic threshold are all likely to have a positive impact on diagnostic accuracy and treatment seeking. This might result in greater screening in substance using populations where there is a known co-morbidity of gambling disorder, more diagnostic efforts and therefore a higher likelihood of being offered interventions for gambling disorder (Petry et al, 2014).

This chapter will provide an overview of the different methods of screening, and structured and clinical assessments for gambling disorder.

Assessment of gambling disorder

Assessments in gambling disorder, as with any addiction - related disorder, can done at 3 levels:

1. Clinical assessment, which happens through a detailed personal interview and mental status examination

2. Screening with the help of instruments
3. Structured instruments for assessment of gambling disorder

Clinical assessment

Clinical assessment of gambling disorder is important to understand both the extent and impact of gambling, and also to help in planning treatment interventions. It involves evaluation of the different facets of gambling, co-morbidities, and temperamental and personality traits. The integrative disordered gambling case conceptualization is one such process used in the clinical assessment of gambling disorder (Slutske, 2006). Our approach draws upon facets of the same, however in the context of the growing evidence for addictive disorders being an extension of developmental psychopathology, we follow the scheme of assessment that is explained below in Figure 1.

Figure 7.1: Scheme of assessment in gambling disorder

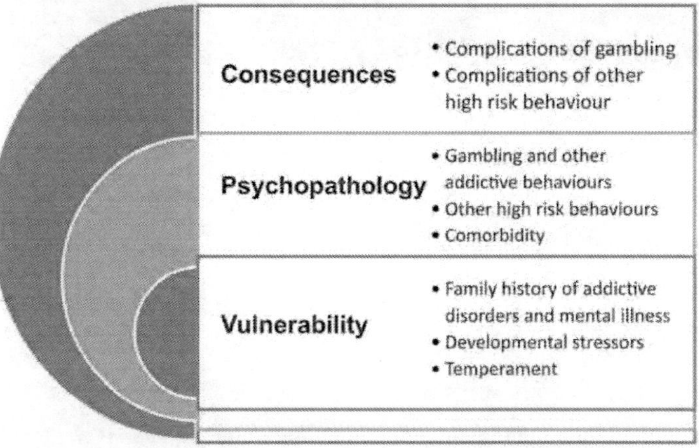

Vulnerability

Evaluation of pre-morbid temperament and personality

The importance of evaluating temperament and personality traits in disordered gamblers is that it gives a clue towards etiology, and helps to understand typologies within disordered gamblers, thus moulding the clinician's approach towards treatment.

Studies have pointed towards high negative and positive emotionality, and low degrees of constraint in disordered gamblers. These higher order traits may act together to contribute to sensation seeking and impulsivity which are noted in disordered gamblers (Rugle, 2013) (See Figure 7.2). These are similar to the profiles associated with alcohol, cannabis, and nicotine dependence (Slutske et al, 2005).

In addition, nearly half (47.9%) of treatment-seeking problem gamblers also report co-morbid personality disorders, specifically narcissistic (16.6%), antisocial (14.0%), avoidant (13.4%), obsessive–compulsive (13.4%), and borderline (13.1%) personality disorders (Dowling et al, 2015). A systematic review and meta-analysis of co-morbid disorders in population - representative samples of problem gamblers showed co-morbidity rates of 29% for antisocial personality disorder (Lorains et al, 2011).

Figure 7.2: A model of personality traits and disordered gambling

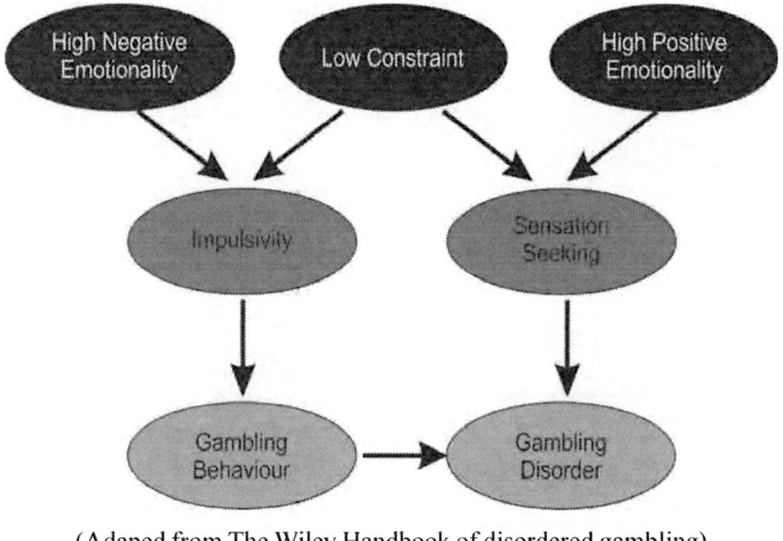

(Adaped from The Wiley Handbook of disordered gambling)

Psychopathology

Description of the gambling problem

This includes:

1. Longitudinal description
   - At what age did you first gamble and what was this first experience like?

- What type of gambling did you first engage in and in what context or situation?
- How did the gambling progress?
- When did you begin gambling frequently or start becoming preoccupied with gambling?
- What was the type and context of gambling at this point?
- At what age did you first begin to consider that gambling was becoming problematic in your life?
- At what point did others in your life have concerns about or criticize your gambling?
- What type of gambling was creating problems?
- Was there ever a period of time when you were winning more than losing or when your gambling was limited or controlled? If so how long did this last?
- What were your life circumstances around the time when gambling began to increase or become problematic?
- Since you began gambling frequently or problematically, have you made any efforts to stop, control or cut back? If so what did you try and how did it work?

2. Current description
   - What are the types of gambling activities you engage in?
   - What are the venues where you gamble?
   - How often do you gamble?
   - How much time and money is spent gambling?

Description of a typical episode of gambling

Such a description is particularly useful when planning cognitive behavioural interventions for disordered gambling. It typically involves describing physical sensations, thoughts and emotions during anticipation of gambling, during gambling itself and in the aftermath.

Evaluation of comorbidity

A systematic review and meta-analysis of co-morbid Axis I disorders in population-representative samples of problem gamblers revealed high rates of psychiatric disorders including nicotine dependence (60%), alcohol and other substance use disorders (58%), mood disorders (38%) and anxiety disorders (37%) (Lorains et al, 2011).

Another systematic review and meta-analysis of co-morbid Axis I disorders in treatment seeking problem gamblers also revealed high rates of co-morbid current (74.8%) and lifetime (75.5%) Axis I disorders. These included current mood disorders (23.1%), alcohol use disorders (21.2), anxiety disorders (17.6%) and substance (non-alcohol) use disorders (7.0%) (Dowling et al, 2015).

The presence of co-morbid disorders in treatment-seekers is associated with an increased severity of gambling behaviour and gambling-related negative consequences (Ladd and Petry, 2003; Hall et al, 2000). It also affects an individual's compliance with treatment, success of treatment, likelihood of relapse and the number of treatment attempts (Kruedelbach et al, 2005; Westphal et al, 2000).

All the above highlight the importance of evaluating for the presence of co-morbid psychiatric disorders.

Consequences

These include a wide range of adverse consequences as a result of gambling.

1. Interpersonal consequences

- What concerns do you have about the impact of gambling on your relationships with family, friends, co-workers, etc.?
- How would you describe ways that gambling has either improved or worsened your family life, friendships, work/career/education, etc.?
- Do you feel or have people close to you commented that you have become more isolated lately?
- How has gambling affected your work/career/education?
- Has your work performance changed lately?
- Have you received any criticism about your performance at work or school recently?
- Has gambling been a distraction to your work or school performance?
- Have you gambled when you should have been working, at school or studying?
- Have you chosen to gamble rather than attend other social activities with friends or family (i.e. parties, holiday activities, etc.)?

- Have you discontinued or stopped doing other activities you used to enjoy because you would rather gamble, or because you don't have the money for these activities?
- Have you avoided talking to any friends or family members due to gambling or owing money?

2. Financial consequences

- How much debt are you in?
- What percentage of your debt would you say is due to your gambling?
- How much money have you borrowed from family or friends and not yet paid back (whether or not you think family members expect repayment)?
- How much, if any, are you behind on any bills?
- Have any services been cancelled due to your inability to pay?
- Have you ever been evicted due to inability to pay rent?
- How many credit cards do you currently have active?
- What is your current credit card balance?
- Have you utilized savings to stay current on payments or pay off debt?
- Have you taken out loans to repay debt related to gambling?
- Have you sold or pawned personal property to pay off debt?

3. Legal consequences

- Have you ever written any bad checks to fund gambling, to pay off debts due to gambling, or to pay necessary expenses because of spending money on gambling?
- Have you forged a signature on someone else's account to obtain money for gambling or to pay debt due to gambling?
- Have you forged a signature on other financial documents to obtain money for gambling or pay debt due to gambling?
- Have you committed fraud to obtain money for gambling or pay debt due to gambling?
- Have you taken money from your work place due to gambling?
- Have you stolen money or property from anyone (including family) or any organization due to gambling?

- Have you not paid or not filed taxes or filed false tax statements due to gambling?
- Have you sold illegal drugs to obtain money for gambling?
- Have you engaged in prostitution to due to gambling?
- Are you concerned about any legal consequences due to your gambling or activities around obtaining money due to gambling?
- Have you operated any illegal gambling operations?

Mental status examination

This is important both from the point of view of assessment of cognitive distortions and biases commonly associated with gambling disorder, and diagnosing co-morbidities like depression which commonly co-exist.

A comprehensive list of cognitive distortions and biases associated with gambling disorder is given below (Toneatto et al, 1997; Fortune and Goodie, 2012) and their identification is of therapeutic importance, particularly in cognitive behavioural therapy.

Magnification of gambling skill

- Overrating one's ability to win at gambling
- Talismanic superstitions – Beliefs that the possession of certain objects increases the probability of winning (e.g. ring, hat)
- Behavioural superstitions – Beliefs that certain actions or rituals can increase the probability of winning (e.g. playing on only certain slot machines or placing smaller bets if they do not throw the dice themselves)
- Cognitive superstitions – Beliefs that certain mental states can affect the probability of winning (e.g. prayer, hope, positive expectancies)
- Interpretative biases
- Attributional biases – Tendency to overestimate dispositional factors (e.g. skills, abilities) to explain wins and to underestimate situational factors (e.g. luck, probability)
- Gambler's fallacy – Belief that a win is due after a series of losses
- Chasing – Belief that the only way to recover financial loss is to continue to gamble
- Anthropomorphism – Attribute human characteristics to non-animate or non-human gambling objects (e.g. slot machine, lottery card, bingo card, horses)

- Learning from losses – Continuing to gamble is highly justifiable because losses are perceived as valuable learning experiences, which can ultimately lead to winning
- Hindsight bias – Retrospectively evaluating gambling decisions as correct or incorrect on the basis of whether they lead to wins or losses
- Temporal telescoping: Belief that wins are actually nearer, temporally, than further, especially if the gambling is relying on superstitious behaviour or gambling systems to win; the gambler makes the additional assumption that they (rather than other gamblers) will win, even if other gamblers have also incurred serious losses and are expecting to win
- Selective memory: Selectively recalling wins, especially large ones, and having difficulty recalling losses
- Predictive skill: Making gambling decisions on the basis of interpretations or meanings assigned to subjectively salient or important cues; cues can be internal (e.g., bodily perceptions, gut sensations, intuitions, feelings) or external (e.g., omens, weather phenomena, serendipitous events) or behaviour by other gamblers

Illusions of control over luck

- Luck can be perceived as an important variable and is regarded as an uncontrollable variable (i.e., luck oscillates between periods of good and bad luck and cannot be manipulated directly), a controllable variable (i.e., luck can be manipulated through superstitious behaviours or systems), a trait variable (i.e., people are characteristically lucky with certain games and unlucky with others), or a contagion (i.e., luck is affected by other areas of their life or by other people)
- Illusory associations: Perceiving illusory associations or assigning causality to salient features of the environment believed to be associated with gambling outcomes (e.g., noticing more frequent winning at night, noticing that certain days of the week are more likely to lead to wins, believing that watching a sports game on television will favour a specific team)

Screening tools for gambling disorder

Gambling disorder is a fairly common disorder and has public health significance. It is thus important to have screening tools to suspect a diagnosis of gambling disorder in non-treatment seeking populations.

There are a large number of screening tools (Table 7.2) for gambling disorder that vary in their length and time required for administration. Most of them have been developed for epidemiological studies and derive or draw on the diagnostic criteria for pathological gambling or gambling disorder as in the psychiatric classificatory manuals such as ICD and DSM. These have been noted to have good sensitivity and specificity in detecting people with problem or pathological gambling.

Table 7.2: Screening instruments for gambling disorder

Detailed screening instruments			
Name	**Description**	**Number of items/ Time frame**	**Interpretation**
South Oaks Gambling Screen (SOGS) (Lesieur and Blume, 1987)	Based on DSM-III criteria for pathological gambling	26 items out of which 20 are scored lifetime, past year, and past 3 months	Score (5 or more) – probable pathological gambler
Problem Gambling Severity Index (PGSI) (Holtgraves, 2009)	Derived from Canadian Problem Gambling Index (31 items)	9 items Past year	Score (8 or more) – Problem gambling with negative consequences and possible loss of control
Massachusetts Gambling Screen (MAGS) (Shaffer et al, 1994)	Based on DSM – IV signs and symptoms of pathological gambling PLUS associated psychological and social problems	31 items 7 items – MAGS classification 12 items – DSM IV classification over past year	Score (0 and 2) – Transitional gambler Score (> 2) – Pathological gambler Score (> 5) – Pathological
National Opinion Research Center DSMIV Screen for Gambling Problems (NODS) (Hodgins, 2004)	DSM-IV diagnostic criteria for pathological gambling	17 items each lifetime and past-year	Score (3 – 4) – Possible pathological gambler Score (5 or more) – Probable pathological

Contd....

Contd....

Brief screening instruments			
Name	**Description**	**Number of items/ Time frame**	**Interpretation**
NODS-CliP (Toce-Gerstein, Gerstein and Volberg, 2009)	Evaluates loss of control, lying and preoccupation	3 items, Yes or No Lifetime	If even 1 item is positive, warrants detailed evaluation
NODS – PERC (Volberg et al, 2011)	Looks for Preoccupation, Escape, Risked Relationships and Chasing	4 items, Yes or No	If even 1 item is positive, warrants detailed evaluation
Brief Biosocial Gambling Screen (BBGS) (Gebauer, LaBrie and Shaffer, 2010)	Based on AUDADIS IV used in NESARC. Evaluates withdrawal, lying and borrowing money	3 items, Yes or No Past year	If even 1 item is positive, warrants detailed evaluation
Lie/Bet scale (Johnson, Hamer and Nora, 1998)	Lies to others about gambling behaviours, or bets more and more money	2 items, Yes or No Lifetime	"Yes" to one or both items indicates PG

Structured instruments for assessment of gambling disorder

Structured instruments find their utility mostly in research but may be also used in clinical practice. They cannot however replace a clinical interview by a qualified psychiatrist with respect to making a diagnosis of gambling disorder. Two such instruments are described briefly below:

Gambling Treatment Outcome Monitoring System (GAMTOMS) (Stinchfield et al, 2007): It is a multidimensional self-report or interview assessment instrument. It incorporates SOGS and also assesses various domains pertaining to treatment planning and outcome monitoring including gambling frequency, mental health, financial problems, legal problems and motivation. Additionally, this system has a ten-item DSM-IV measure that is relevant for diagnostic purposes.

Diagnostic Interview for Gambling Schedule (DIGS) (Fortune and Goodie, 2010): This instrument includes demographics, gambling involvement, treatment history, onset of gambling, gambling frequency, amounts of money bet and lost, sources of borrowed money, financial problems, legal problems, mental health screen, other impulse disorders, medical status, family and social functioning, and diagnostic symptoms (lifetime and past year). It has 20 items in total and is based on DSM-IV TR diagnostic criteria. If the respondent endorses either of the two items per criterion, the criterion is considered met.

Scales for assessment of severity and treatment response in gambling disorder.

Yale Brown Obsessive Compulsive Scale adapted for Pathological Gambling (PG-YBOCS) (Pallanti et al, 2005): This scale was developed to measure the severity and change in severity of pathological gambling symptoms. The PG-YBOCS is a 10-item clinician-administered questionnaire that measures the severity of pathological gambling over a recent time interval (usually within the past one/two weeks). The first five questions assess urges and thoughts associated with pathological gambling, whereas the last five questions assess the behavioural component of the disorder. The PG-YBOCS showed high validity and reliability for total score, item-total correlations, and for each subscale (thoughts/urges and behaviour) and is also sensitive to change in pathological gambling severity.

Gambling Symptom Assessment Scale (G-SAS) (Kim et al, 2009): It is a 12-item self - rated scale designed to assess gambling symptom severity and change during treatment. Each item scale has a score ranging from 0 to 4. All items ask for an average symptom based on the past 7 days.

Items 1 to 4 ask for the average urge (only gambling urges, excludes other urges), symptom severity, frequency, duration and control; items 5 to 7 ask for the average frequency, duration and control of thoughts associated with gambling (excludes other thoughts); item 8 asks for the time spent on gambling or gambling related behaviour, item 9 asks for the anticipatory tension and/ or excitement caused by an imminent gambling act; item 10 asks for the excitement and pleasure associated with winning, item 11 asks for emotional distress (mental pain, anguish, shame, guilt, or embarrassment) caused by gambling and item 12 asks for personal trouble (relationship, financial, legal, job, medical or health) caused by gambling.

Conclusion

It is important to screen for gambling disorder and evaluate it, particularly in those with substance use disorders, depression and externalizing disorders.

Although screening tools have good sensitivity and specificity, a definitive diagnosis requires detailed clinical evaluation which covers an in depth description of gambling, its psychosocial consequences, presence of co-morbidities and evaluation of the pre-morbid temperament and personality.

Key points

- Epidemiological studies estimate the prevalence of past-year adult pathological gambling to be between 1.1 and 3.5%, and between 6 and 9 percent in young people. However, it remains under-recognized in clinical practice.
- Gambling disorder's inclusion in the section on addictive disorders in DSM V and change in its diagnostic threshold are likely to have a positive impact on diagnostic accuracy and treatment seeking.
- Assessment in gambling disorder is best done at 3 levels: clinical assessment (personal interview and mental status examination), screening with the help of instruments and structured instruments for assessment.
- Identification of cognitive distortions and biases associated with gambling disorder is an important part of assessment as it is necessary for CBT of gambling disorder.
- Problematic gamblers have high rates of comorbid psychiatric disorders including nicotine dependence, alcohol and other substance use disorders, mood disorders and anxiety disorders, and this needs to be an important part of the assessment.

References

American Psychiatric Association. (2013). Diagnostic and statistical manual of mental disorders (5th Ed.). Arlington, VA: American Psychiatric Publishing.

Barnes, G. M., Welte, J. W., Hoffman, J. H., Tidwell, M. C. (2010). Comparisons of gambling and alcohol use among college students and non - college young people in the United States. *Journal of American College Health*, 24; 58(5):443-52.

Benegal, V. (2013). Gambling experiences, problems and policy in India: a historical analysis. *Addiction*. 1; 108(12):2062-7.

Dowling, N. A., Cowlishaw, S., Jackson, A. C., Merkouris, S. S., Francis, K. L., Christensen, D. R. (2015). Prevalence of psychiatric co-morbidity in treatment-seeking problem gamblers: a systematic review and meta-analysis. *Australian & New Zealand Journal of Psychiatry*. 49(6):519-39.

Fortune, E.E. & Goodie, A.S. (2010). Comparing the utility of a modified Diagnostic Interview for Gambling Severity (DIGS) with the South Oaks Gambling Screen (SOGS) as a research screen in college students. *Journal of Gambling Studies*, 1; 26(4):639-44.

Fortune, E. E. & Goodie, A. S. (2012). Cognitive distortions as a component and treatment focus of pathological gambling: a review. *Psychology of Addictive Behaviours*, 26(2):298.

Gebauer, L., LaBrie, R., Shaffer, H. J. (2010). Optimizing DSM-IV-TR classification accuracy: a brief biosocial screen for detecting current gambling disorders among gamblers in the general household population. *The Canadian Journal of Psychiatry*. 55(2):82-90.

Hall, G. W., Carriero, N. J., Takushi, R. Y., Montoya, I. D., Preston, K. L., Gorelick, D. A. (2000). Pathological gambling among cocaine-dependent outpatients. *American Journal of Psychiatry*. 157(7):1127-33.

Hodgins, D. C. (2004). Using the NORC DSM Screen for Gambling Problems as an outcome measure for pathological gambling: psychometric evaluation. *Addictive Behaviours*, 29(8):1685-90.

Holtgraves, T. (2009). Evaluating the problem gambling severity index. *Journal of Gambling Studies*, 25(1):105.

Johnson, E. E., Hamer, R. M., Nora, R. M. (1998). The Lie/Bet Questionnaire for screening pathological gamblers: a follow-up study. *Psychological Reports*, 83(3 suppl):1219-24.

Kim, S. W., Grant, J. E., Potenza, M. N., Blanco, C., Hollander, E. (2009). The Gambling Symptom Assessment Scale (G-SAS): a reliability and validity study. *Psychiatry Research*, 166(1):76-84.

Kruedelbach, N., Walker, H. I., Chapman, H. A., Haro, G., Mateu, C., Leal, C. (2005). Comorbidity on disorders with loss of impulse-control: pathological gambling, addictions and personality disorders. *Actasespañolas de Psiquiatría*, 34(2):76-82.

Ladd, G. T. & Petry, N. M. (2003). A comparison of pathological gamblers with and without substance abuse treatment histories. *Experimental and Clinical Psychopharmacology*, 11(3):202.

Lesieur, H. R. & Blume, S. B. (1987). The South Oaks Gambling Screen (SOGS): A new instrument for the identification of pathological gamblers. *American Journal of Psychiatry*, 144(9):1184 – 88.

Lorains, F. K., Cowlishaw, S., Thomas, S. A. (2011). Prevalence of comorbid disorders in problem and pathological gambling: Systematic review and meta analysis of population surveys. *Addiction*, 106(3):490-8.

Pallanti, S., DeCaria, C. M., Grant, J. E., Urpe, M., Hollander, E. (2005). Reliability and validity of the pathological gambling adaptation of the Yale-Brown Obsessive-compulsive Scale (PG-YBOCS). *Journal of Gambling Studies*, 21(4):431-43.

Petry, N. M., Blanco, C., Auriacombe, M., Borges, G., Bucholz, K., Crowley, T. J. et al. (2014). An overview of and rationale for changes proposed for pathological gambling in DSM-5. Journal of gambling studies/cosponsored by the National Council on Problem Gambling and Institute for the Study of Gambling and Commercial Gaming. 30(2):493.

Rugle, L. (2013). Case Conceptualization with Clients Presenting with Disordered Gambling. The Wiley-Blackwell Handbook of Disordered Gambling. 132-64.

Shaffer, H. J., LaBrie, R., Scanlan, K. M., Cummings, T. N. (1994). Pathological gambling among adolescents: Massachusetts gambling screen (MAGS). *Journal of Gambling Studies*, 10(4):339-62.

Shaffer, H. J., Hall, M. N., Vander Bilt, J. (1999). Estimating the prevalence of disordered gambling behaviour in the United States and Canada: a research synthesis. *American Journal of Public Health*, 89(9):1369-76.

Shaffer, H. J. & Hall, M. N. (2001). Updating and refining prevalence estimates of disordered gambling behaviour in the United States and Canada. *Canadian Journal of Public Health*, 92(3):168.

Slutske, W. S., Caspi, A., Moffitt, T. E., Poulton, R. (2005). Personality and problem gambling: A prospective study of a birth cohort of young adults. *Archives of General Psychiatry*, 62(7):769-75.

Slutske, W. S. (2006). Natural recovery and treatment-seeking in pathological gambling: Results of two US national surveys. *American Journal of Psychiatry*, 163(2):297-302.

Stinchfield, R., Winters, K. C., Botzet, A., Jerstad, S., Breyer, J. (2007). Development and

psychometric evaluation of the gambling treatment outcome monitoring system (GAMTOMS). *Psychology of Addictive Behaviours*, 21(2):174.
Toneatto, T., Blitz-Miller, T., Calderwood, K., Dragonetti, R., Tsanos, A. (1997). Cognitive distortions in heavy gambling. *Journal of Gambling Studies*. 13(3):253-66.
Toce-Gerstein, M., Gerstein, D. R., Volberg, R. A. (2009). The NODS–CLiP: A rapid screen for adult pathological and problem gambling. *Journal of Gambling Studies*. 25(4):541-55.
Volberg, R. A., Munck, I. M., Petry, N. M. (2011). A quick and simple screening method for pathological and problem gamblers in addiction programs and practices. *The American Journal on Addictions*, 20(3):220-7.
Welte, J. W., Barnes, G. M., Wieczorek, W. F., Tidwell, M. C., Parker, J. (2002). Gambling participation in the US—results from a national survey. *Journal of Gambling S tudies*, 18(4):313-37.
Westphal, J. R., Johnson, L. J., Stodghill, S., Stevens, L. (2000). Gambling in the south: implications for physicians. *Southern Medical Journal*, 93(9):850-8.

Chapter 8

Treatment of gambling disorder

Jayant Mahadevan and Arun Kandasamy

Introduction

Many pharmacological and psychosocial interventions have been studied in patients with gambling disorder. These have yielded variable outcomes. Counter intuitively, there is also evidence that a significant proportion of problem or pathological gamblers never seek treatment and a large number achieve recovery without any formal treatment (Slutske, 2006).

Treatment of gambling disorder

Majority of patients with gambling disorder are encountered in psychiatric outpatient treatment settings. The need for inpatient care in these patients would usually be related to the presence of other co-morbidities like depression, suicidality or substance use disorders.

Treatment seeking amongst patients with gambling disorder is fairly low with estimates of 7 to 12 % ever having sought treatment or attended Gamblers Anonymous meetings (Slutske, 2006). Reasons for this may include shame, guilt or denial of problems (Cunningham, 2005; Suurvali, Hodgins and Cunningham, 2010). However it may also be attributable to the fact that anywhere between 36 and 39% of patients with a lifetime diagnosis of gambling disorder do not experience current gambling - related problems despite the low rates of treatment seeking and many had natural recovery (Slutske, 2006). This points to the fact that at least in a sub-group of patients, gambling disorder may not have a chronic or persistent course.

Treatment of gambling disorder generally requires a combination of approaches, encompassing both pharmacological and psychological interventions.

Pharmacological treatment of gambling disorder

Despite numerous controlled trials of multiple pharmacotherapies, there is currently no FDA-approved pharmacotherapy for treatment of gambling disorder.

The rationale behind selection of pharmacotherapy has been based on understanding gambling disorder as a product of an addictive process, an obsessive – compulsive spectrum disorder or emotional dysregulation. The heterogeneity inherent in the population of disordered gamblers has probably resulted in the mixed results with regards to research into pharmacotherapy.

The following section lists various agents employed in the pharmacological treatment of gambling disorder classified based on both class of drug and receptor or neurotransmitter being targeted. It will also list relevant research into their efficacy and their recommendation for use.

Opioidergic pharmacotherapies – naltrexone and nalmefene

There have been several double-blind, placebo controlled trials of the opioid antagonists naltrexone and nalmefene that suggest clinical efficacy over placebo (Table 8.1). A recent meta-analysis of pharmacological interventions for gambling disorder which included 14 trials with 1024 participants demonstrated a small but significant benefit of opiate receptor antagonists as compared to placebo (Bartley and Bloch, 2013). On the weight of current research, they may thus be considered to be the first line agents in pharmacotherapy for gambling disorder. However, it may be most effective in treating gambling disorder among individuals who are family-history positive for alcoholism.

Table 8.1: Opioidergic pharmacotherapies in gambling disorder

Study	N	Dose and duration	Design	Results
Kim et al (2001)	89	Naltrexone mean dose – 188 mg/ day; Duration: 12 weeks (1-week single blind placebo lead-in followed by an 11- week double-blind naltrexone or placebo trial)	Randomized double blind Placebo controlled	Outcome: Gambling symptom assessment scale (G-SAS), Patient and Clinician rated (Clinical Global Impression Improvement) CGI – I Naltrexone is significantly superior to placebo

Cont...

Cont...

Grant, Kim and Hartman, (2008)	77	Naltrexone dose range – 50 - 150 mg/day; Duration: 18 weeks	Randomized double blind Placebo controlled	Outcome: Scores of urge and behaviour subscales of the PG YBOCS and (G-SAS). Naltrexone is significantly superior to placebo
Toneatto, Brands and Selby (2009)	52	Naltrexone mean dose: 100 ± 59 mg/day; Duration: 12 weeks (1-week single blind placebo lead in followed by an 11- week double-blind naltrexone or placebo trial)	Randomized double blind Placebo controlled for co-morbid alcohol dependence and pathological gambling	Outcome: Gambling frequency and expenditures, Alcohol quantity and frequency No difference between two groups on outcome measures
Kovanen et al (2016)	101	As-needed placebo or naltrexone (50 mg) and psychosocial support Duration: 20 weeks	Randomized double blind Placebo controlled	Outcome: PG-YBOCS, Thoughts/urges and behaviour subscales of PGYBOCS, gambling frequency and highest daily expenditure No difference between two groups on outcome measures
Grant et al 2006	207	Nalmefene dose range: 25, 50 and 100 mg/day; Duration:16 weeks	Randomized double blind Placebo controlled	Outcome: PG-YBOCS Nalmefene 25mg and 50mg superior to placebo. More tolerable than 100mg Dropout rate – 66%

Cont...

Cont...

Grant et al 2010	233	Nalmefene dose range: 20 and 40 mg/day; Duration: 16weeks (1-week single blind placebo lead-in followed by double-blind nalmefene or placebo trial)	Randomized double blind Placebo controlled	Outcome: PG-YBOCS, Thoughts/urges and behaviour subscales of PG-YBOCS No differences between groups noted Dropout rate – 46%

Selective Serotonin Reuptake Inhibitors

Although alterations in serotonergic functioning among individuals with gambling disorder have long been posited, findings from clinical trials thus far suggest limited efficacy of selective serotonin reuptake inhibitors (SSRIs) for the treatment of gambling disorder.

Four different SSRIs namely fluvoxamine, sertraline, escitalopram and paroxetine have been studied with mixed or negative findings (Table 8.2). Large rates of placebo response and high dropout rates are noted in studies.

Table 8.2: Selective serotonin reuptake inhibitors in gambling disorder

Study	N	Dose and Duration	Design	Results
Hollander et al 2000	15	Fluvoxamine mean dose 195 mg/day; Duration: 16 weeks	Double blind cross-over design Placebo controlled	Outcome: overall score in PGYBOCS and PG-CGI Fluvoxamine is superior to Placebo
Blanco et al 2002	32	Fluvoxamine mean dose 200 mg/day; Duration: 24 weeks	Randomized double blind Placebo controlled	Outcome: Reduction in money and time spent in gambling per week Fluvoxamine is not significantly superior to placebo High (59%) placebo-response rate

Cont...

Cont...

Dannon et al 2005	31	Fluvoxamine and Topiramate Duration: 12 weeks	Randomized blind rater comparison	Outcome: PGYBOCS, CGI – I Improvements in both Fluvoxamine and Topiramate treatment groups between baseline and 12 weeks. No differences between groups
Kim et al 2002	45	Paroxetine with dose range: 20–60 mg/day; Duration: 8 weeks	Randomized double blind Placebo controlled	Outcome: Scores on G – SAS and CGI Paroxetine is superior to placebo
Grant et al 2003	76	Paroxetine 10–60 mg/day; duration:16 weeks	Randomized double blind Placebo controlled	Outcome: Overall score in PGYBOCS, G – SAS an CGI Paroxetine is not significantly superior to placebo
Saiz-Ruiz et al, 2005	60	Sertraline 50–150 mg/day; Duration: 24 weeks	Randomized double blind, flexible dose Placebo controlled	Outcome: Criteria for Control of Pathological Gambling Questionnaire (CCPGQ) Sertraline is not significantly superior to placebo
Grant and Potenza, 2006	13	Escitalopram mean dose 25 mg/ day; Duration: 20 weeks	Open label trial for 12 weeks then Double-blind Placebo controlled for 8 weeks for PG with comorbid anxiety	Outcome: overall score in PGYBOCS and score on HAM-A Escitalopram is superior to placebo

Mood stabilizers – Lithium and Valproate

Initial studies suggested some efficacy of mood stabilizers, lithium and valproate in treating gambling disorder and mood stabilizer treatment is recommended for the treatment of GD among individuals with a co-occurring bipolar spectrum disorder. However, most of these studies did not have a placebo group. A 10 week randomized double blind placebo controlled study of sustained release – lithium carbonate showed that lithium at a mean dose of 1170 mg/day was significantly superior to placebo in terms of improvements in PG – YBOCS and CGI – S (Hollander et al, 2005).

Dopaminergic pharmacotherapies – Bupropion and Olanzapine

While pre-clinical data points to a role of dopamine in the pathogenesis of gambling disorder, controlled trials of dopaminergic pharmacotherapies suggest limited clinical utility of these medications (Table 8.3).

Table 8.3: Dopaminergic pharmacotherapies in Gambling Disorder

Study	N	Dose and Duration	Design	Results
McElroy et al, 2008	42	Olanzapine 2.5–15 mg/day; Duration: 12 weeks	Randomized double blind Placebo controlled	Outcome: Change in obsessions subscale of the PG – YBOCS Olanzapine is not significantly superior to placebo
Fong et al, 2008	23	Olanzapine 2.5–10 mg/day; Duration: 7 weeks	Randomized double blind Placebo controlled	Outcome: Self-reported urges for gambling, frequency of gambling behaviour, and self reported mood and anxiety levels Olanzapine is not significantly superior to placebo

Cont...

Cont...

Black et al, 2007	39	Bupropion (NDRI) mean dose 325 mg/day; Duration: 12 weeks	Randomized double blind Placebo controlled	Outcome: PG – YBOCS, G – SAS, CGI – I Bupropion is not significantly superior to placebo

Glutamatergic pharmacotherapies

An imbalance in glutamate homeostasis – the relative ratio of synaptic versus non synaptic glutamate – may inhibit successful prefrontal cortical control over limbic regions such as the nucleus accumbens, resulting in increased reward seeking behaviours. This has led to controlled trials exploring the efficacy of the same in gambling disorder which have turned up some promising findings, particularly for N – Acetyl Cysteine (Table 8.4).

Table 8.4: Glutamatergic pharmacotherapies in gambling disorder

Study	N	Dose and Duration	Design	Results
Grant et al, 2007	27	N-acetyl cysteine (NAC) Mean effective dose: 1477mg/day; Duration: 14 weeks	Open label trial for 8 weeks then double blind trial for the next 6 weeks	Outcome. PG-YBOCS total score NAC is superior to placebo
Grant et al, 2014	28	N-acetyl cysteine (NAC) dose: 1200- 3000 mg/day; Duration:12 weeks	Randomized double blind Placebo controlled with co-morbid nicotine dependence	Outcome: Scores on Fagerström test for nicotine dependence and PGYBOCS total score During the 3month follow up, NAC was superior to placebo on PG severity and NAC facilitates long term behavioural therapy

Cont...

Cont...

Grant et al. 2010	29	Memantine mean effective dose of 23 mg/day Duration: 10 weeks	Open label study	Outcome: PGYBOCS total score and also gambling frequency/duration Improved scores than the baseline
Thomas et al. 2011	17	Amantadine mean dose of 200 mg/day	Open label placebo controlled study with comorbid Parkinson's Disease	Outcome: PGYBOCS total score and daily expenditure reduction Amantadine is better than placebo
Berlin et al, 2013	42	Topiramate 25–300 mg/day; Duration:14 weeks	Randomized double blind Placebo controlled	Outcome: Change in obsessions subscale of the PG- YBOCS and scores on Barratt's impulsiveness scale Topiramate is not significantly superior to placebo

Brain stimulation techniques

There is some evidence for the use of brain stimulation methods, particularly repetitive transcranial magnetic stimulation (rTMS) and transcranial direct current stimulation (tDCS) in treating gambling disorder (Table 8.5). This evidence stems mainly from their role in improved decision making by healthy individuals in gambling tasks.

Table 8.5: Brain stimulation techniques in gambling disorder

Study	**N**	**Dose and Duration**	**Design**	**Results**
Gay et al. 2017	22	Real or sham treatment with high frequency rTMS over the left dorsolateral	Randomized sham-controlled crossover trial	Outcome: Cue induced gambling craving (from 0 to 100) before and after viewing a

Cont...

Cont...

		prefrontal cortex (DLPFC) followed a week later by the other type of treatment.		gambling video – Before and after each rTMS session PG YBOCS - Gambling behaviour before and 7 days after each rTMS session Real rTMS significantly decreased cue-induced craving, No significant effect was observed on gambling behaviour.

Psychological treatment of gambling disorder

Research in the area of psychological treatment for gambling disorder is perhaps better developed as opposed to pharmacological treatment. Several psychological treatment options for gamblers have been explored.

These include:

- Brief and motivational interventions
- Cognitive behaviour therapy (CBT) – Individual and Group
- Self-help and peer support: Gamblers Anonymous (GA)
- Family interventions
- Combination of psychosocial interventions

Brief and motivational interventions

Motivational approaches attempt to address client ambivalence towards change. This may include weighing the advantages and disadvantages of changing their gambling behaviour and providing personalized and/or normative feedback. A Cochrane review of psychological therapies for pathological gambling/gambling disorder found that there were three eligible randomized trials which compared brief or motivational interventions with control conditions. It provided evidence of some beneficial effects from therapy in terms of less financial loss from gambling at 0 to 3 months post-treatment and less frequent gambling at 9 to 12months follow-up, but almost no effects on other symptoms of pathological and problem gambling (Cowlishaw et al, 2012). Table 8.6 summarizes studies which utilized brief and motivational interviewing techniques as part of their intervention.

Table 8.6: Brief and motivational interventions for gambling disorder

Study	N	Study design, number and duration of sessions	Results
Carlbringet al, 2010	150 self-recruited participants 127 (that attended at least one treatment session) included in the analyses	Group CBT (eight sessions) vs. motivational interviewing (four sessions) vs. no treatment control group Six- and 12-month follow-up	Outcome: Severity of PG, symptoms of anxiety and depression CBT=MI>Control group
Diskin & Hodgins, 2009	81 media recruited participants (>40% female) enrolled 69 completed 12month follow-up	Single session in-person motivational interviewing vs. control interview One-, three-, six and 12- month follow-up	Outcome: Gambling severity MI significantly better than control interview Improvement persisted after 12 Months
Petry et al, 2009	117 college student problem and pathological gamblers 114 completed Week 6 evaluation 113 completed 9-month follow-up	10 minutes of Brief advice vs. 1 session Motivational enhancement therapy (MET) vs. 1 MET + 3 CBT sessions vs. assessment only no treatment control group 6 week and nine-month follow-up	Outcome: Gambling assessed at baseline, week 6, and month 9 using the Addiction Severity Index Gambling (ASI-G) module. All treatment conditions provided significant symptom improvement although MET had the most significant effect relative to the control group

Cont...

Cont...

Petry et al, 2008	180 problem gamblers	10 minutes of Brief advice vs. 1 session Motivational enhancement therapy (MET) vs. 1 MET + 3 CBT sessions vs. assessment only no treatment control group 6 week and nine-month follow-up	Outcome: Gambling assessed at baseline, week 6, and month 9 using the Addiction Severity Index Gambling (ASI-G) module Brief Advice only significantly decreased gambling between baseline and week 6, and was associated with clinically significant reductions in gambling at month 9

Cognitive behaviour therapies

These consist of both cognitive and behavioural therapies. Cognitive therapies focus on correcting erroneous beliefs about gambling, as well as biased information processing. A list of these cognitive distortions and biases are listed in the previous chapter. Associated therapies may attempt to correct these misconceptions, such as through use of evidencc to demonstrate independence of play.

Behavioural therapies, in contrast, are based on assumptions that gambling is a maladaptive learned behaviour. Early exposure to gambling may lead to initiation of the behaviour, which is maintained through conditioning processes. Positive reinforcement may involve a variable-ratio schedule of financial gain, along with negative reinforcement from escape of negative emotional states. Arousal from gambling may become associated with gambling-related external stimuli, and this may also maintain the behaviour. Behavioural therapies are typically based on principles of classical and operant conditioning, and can include aversive therapy, systematic desensitisation and behavioural counselling. Behavioural interventions can also include activity planning, problem-solving training, and social skills and communication training. Cognitive behaviour therapy (CBT) combines various aspects of these therapeutic techniques. It may be delivered both individually and in groups.

A Cochrane review of psychological therapies for pathological gambling/ gambling disorder found that there were eleven eligible randomized trials which compared CBT with control conditions. It provided support for the short-term efficacy of CBT where, relative to controls participants randomised to CBT demonstrated reduced gambling symptom severity, financial loss from gambling and less frequent gambling at 0 to 3 months post-treatment. They also demonstrated reduced rates of diagnoses of pathological gambling and symptoms of depression and anxiety (Cowlishaw et al, 2012). Table 8.7 lists some of the important studies that have looked into CBT for gambling disorder.

Table 8.7: Cognitive behavioural interventions for gambling disorder

Study	N	Study design, number and duration of sessions	Results
Sylvain, Ladouceur & Boisvert, 1997	40 enrolled	Randomized controlled trial, Cognitive therapy (CT) + relapse prevention vs. wait list (WL) 30 sessions with six-month follow up	Outcome: Gambling symptom assessment scale to measure gambling severity CT is better than WL control
Ladouceret al, 2001	88 enrolled	Randomized controlled trial Cognitive therapy + relapse prevention vs. wait list 20 sessions with 12 month follow up	Outcome: Gambling symptom assessment scale to measure gambling severity CT is better than WL control
Ladouceuret al, 2003	81 enrolled	Randomized controlled trial Group cognitive therapy (GCT) + relapse prevention vs. wait list 10 weeks with two-year follow up	Outcome: Gambling criteria based on structured interview GCT vs. WL: 65 percent no longer met PG criteria vs. 20 percent on wait list
Melville et al, 2004	32 enrolled (>80% females)	Randomized controlled trial Group CBT, Group + interactive written	Outcome: Gambling criteria based on structured interview and treatment

Cont...

Cont...

		assignments (mapping) vs. waitlist control Two 90-minute sessions each week for eight weeks Combined group included co-morbid mood disorders	retention Combined treatment is better in terms of reduction of GD symptoms Co-morbidity reduced treatment retention
Petry et al, 2006	231 enrolled; 181 completed	Randomized controlled trial Manualized CBT in individual counselling vs. CBT workbook vs. GA referral Eight sessions with one year follow-up	Outcome: Abstinence from gambling or reduction in gambling frequency at the end of the session Individual CBT> CBT workbook> GA referral At the end of 1 year: no difference amongst treatment groups
Dowling, Smith & Thomas, 2007	56 female pathological gamblers with electronic gaming machine gambling problems were enrolled	Randomized controlled trial Individually administered CBT vs Group administered CBT vs Wait list control 12 sessions with 6 month follow up	Outcome: Frequency, duration, amount of money inserted and expenditure gambling, measured using diary records Both individual and group CBT were better than control groups on improvement of gambling measures
Grant et al, 2009	68 individuals were randomised to groups 44 were assessed at end of 6 months 63.2% women	Randomized controlled trial Imaginal desensitization + MI (IDMI) vs GA referral (Waitlist	Outcome: PGYBOCS; G-SAS; CGI-severity scale IDMI was superior to GA referral in acute treatment of

Cont...

Cont...

		control) 6 sessions over 8 weeks 6 month follow up, where those randomized to GA were also offered IDMI	PG Significant reductions in PG urges and behaviour were maintained for 6 months
Marceaux & Melville, 2011	38 individuals were allocated to groups. 33 of these participants completed treatment (or wait-list control)	Randomized controlled trial Twelve-Step Facilitated (TSF) Group Therapy vs Cognitive-Behavioural Group Therapy with Mapping (CBGT mapping) vs Waitlist control 16 sessions over 8 weeks with 6 month follow up	Outcome: DSM-IV criteria interview (past month timeframe), Timeline Follow Back (frequency of gambling, money spent gambling and time spent gambling) TSF and Bitmapping groups had treatment gains following the 8-week intervention and at 6 months
Oei, Raylu & Casey, 2010	102 enrolled, 40 completed 6 - month follow up	Randomized controlled trial Individual CBT vs group CBT 28 of these participants were randomly allocated to a 6-week waitlist control condition prior to receiving the designated treatment. Single 2 hour session for 6 weeks with follow up at 6 months.	Outcomes: Gambling Related Cognitions Scale; Gambling Urge Scale; Average amount gambled per day; Frequency of gambling measured using 5 point ordinal scales Both Individual and Group CBT better than waitlist.

Gamblers Anonymous

Gamblers Anonymous (GA) describes itself as 'a fellowship of men and women who share their experience, strength and hope with each other that they may solve their common problem and help others to recover from a gambling problem' (Gamblers Anonymous, 1984).

Unlike Alcoholics Anonymous (AA), healthcare professionals, patients and gamblers' families are less aware of Gamblers Anonymous (GA). GA is a freely available psychological group intervention for gambling addiction.

Jim W from Los Angeles, USA founded GA in 1957 based on the principles 12 step program of AA. Although GA started in the US it soon took off in several other countries. At present in India, there are only a handful (less than ten) of GA meetings taking place regularly in the country, and these too are only in the big cities of India.

Basic guiding principles of Gamblers Anonymous

The key guiding principles of GA are: it is a fellowship programme; it uses a disease model for compulsive gambling; believes that no cure, only recovery/ control, is possible; recommends total abstinence, not controlled gambling; is not religious but spiritual; considers belief in a higher power to be essential; is a lifelong endeavour; maintains that anonymity is key; encourages personal and spiritual growth; focuses on repeatedly working through the twelve steps; has no fees for membership; has no socio - political or religious affiliation; and it is a way of life.

Table 8.8: The 12 steps Gamblers Anonymous 12 steps

1.	We admitted we were powerless over gambling – that our lives had become unmanageable.
2.	We came to believe that a power greater than ourselves could restore us to a normal way of thinking and living
3.	We made a decision to turn our will and our lives over to the care of this Power of our own understanding
4.	We made a searching and fearless moral and financial inventory of ourselves.
5.	We admitted to ourselves and to another human being the exact nature of our wrongs.
6.	We were entirely ready to have these defects of character removed.
7.	We humbly ask God (of our understanding) to remove our shortcomings.
8.	We made a list of all persons we had harmed and became willing to make amends to them all.
9.	We made direct amends to such people wherever possible, except when to do so would injure them or others.
10.	We continued to take personal inventory and when we were wrong promptly admitted it.

11. Sought through prayer and meditation to improve our conscious contact with God (as we understand him) praying only for knowledge of His will for us and the power to carry that out.
12. Having made an effort to practice these principles in all our affairs, we tried to carry this message to other compulsive gamblers. (Gamblers Anonymous 1984, with permission).

Working through these twelve steps is integral to the gambler's recovery. Although the emphasis, at least initially, is very much on getting the gambler to attend 90 meetings in 90 days, the first 90 days are merely the start of their recovery journey. For further reading, refer to the 'The Blue Book' (Gamblers Anonymous 1984).

GA and other treatments

GA is perfectly compatible with other psychological and/or pharmacological interventions. Psychological interventions that could be offered alongside GA include cognitive behavioural treatments and family interventions. One possible criticism of GA is that it hasn't been subjected to rigorous scientific research such as randomised controlled trials, hence there is lack of evidence that it works. However anecdotal evidence is aplenty that GA is a useful intervention and has helps many gamblers and their families

Gam-Anon and Gam-A-Teen

Gam-Anon is a fellowship for family members (usually spouses) and friends of compulsive gamblers and Gam-A-Teen is a similar programme for children of compulsive gamblers.

Individualizing treatment for gambling disorder

Several authors have attempted to develop typologies of problem gambling in an attempt to understand the heterogeneity inherent in this population with a view to ultimately develop more effective treatments.

The most well validated typology is Blaszczynski and Nower's (2002) pathways model, which proposes three major entry pathways into problem gambling.

Behaviourally conditioned problem gamblers have little psychopathology and develop problem gambling as a consequence of the highly addictive reinforcement schedule of gambling. They may respond to brief interventions using psycho-education and basic cognitive therapy designed to correct irrational beliefs.

Emotionally vulnerable problem gamblers have a biological and emotional vulnerability to gambling with high levels of depression and/or anxiety. They gamble as a form of emotional escape. They usually need more extensive CBT focusing on problem solving and stress reduction. They may also benefit from SSRIs for depression and anxiety. Antisocial problem gamblers are characterised by a history of impulsivity and antisocial behaviour, and have neurological and neurochemical dysfunction. They may need intensive CBT and medications for externalizing disorders including mood stabilizers or stimulants and impulse control training (Blaszczynski & Nower, 2002; Milosevic & Ledgerwood, 2010). Another typology classifies problem gamblers into impulsive, obsessive compulsive and addictive subtypes with treatment chosen accordingly (Dannon et al, 2006). The clinical utility of treatment based on these typologies has not yet been systematically evaluated and would need to be looked into in future studies.

Conclusion

Treatment options for gambling disorder include both pharmacotherapy and psychotherapy. In pharmacotherapy, the maximum evidence is for opiate receptor antagonists namely naltrexone and nalmefene although these are not licensed for use. There are also promising results with N – Acetyl Cysteine. Psychotherapy, whether individual or in group format is the mainstay of treatment and there is robust evidence for both cognitive behavioural interventions and brief motivational interventions. Future studies in this field need to look at defining clinical and/or biological subtypes, developing newer pharmacological interventions and devising methods to individualize treatment for gambling disorder.

Key points

- Those with gambling disorder are very reluctant to seek treatment; reasons include shame, guilt or denial of problems.
- Treatment of gambling disorder requires a combination of pharmacological and psychological interventions.
- Despite numerous controlled trials of multiple pharmacotherapies, there is currently no FDA-approved drug for the treatment of gambling disorder. Opioidergic drugs such as naltrexone and nalmefene, Selective Serotonin Reuptake Inhibitors, mood stabilizers such as valproate and lithium, dopaminergic pharmacotherapies such as bupropion and olanzapine and glutamatergic pharmacotherapies have all been tried, with best evidence for naltrexone and nalmefene.
- Psychological treatments for gambling disorder have been more researched and better developed; these include brief and motivational interventions, cognitive behaviour therapy, Gamblers Anonymous and family interventions.

References

Bartley, C.A. & Bloch, M. H. (2013). Meta-analysis: pharmacological treatment of pathological gambling. *Expert Review of Neurotherapeutics*, 13(8):887-94.

Berlin, H. A., Braun, A., Simeon, D., Koran, L. M., Potenza, M. N., McElroy, S. L.et al. (2013). A double-blind, placebo-controlled trial of topiramate for pathological gambling. *The World Journal of Biological Psychiatry* 14(2):121-8.

Black, D. W., Arndt, S., Coryell, W. H., Argo, T., Forbush, K. T., Shaw, M. C. (2007). Bupropion in the treatment of pathological gambling: a randomized, double-blind, placebo-controlled, flexible-dose study. *Journal of Clinical Psychopharmacology* 27(2):143-50.

Blanco, C., Petkova, E., Ibáñez, A., Sáiz-Ruiz, J. (2002). A pilot placebo-controlled study of fluvoxamine for pathological gambling. *Annals of Clinical Psychiatry*, 14(1):9-15.

Blaszczynski, A. & Nower, L. (2002). A pathways model of problem and pathological gambling. *Addiction*, 97(5):487-99.

Carlbring, P., Jonsson, J., Josephson, H., Forsberg, L. (2010). Motivational interviewing versus cognitive behavioural group therapy in the treatment of problem and pathological gambling: A randomized controlled trial. *Cognitive Behaviour Therapy*. 39(2):92-103.

Cunningham, J. A. (2005). Little use of treatment among problem gamblers. *Psychiatric Services*, 56(8):1024-a.

Dannon, P. N., Lowengrub, K., Gonopolski, Y., Musin, E., Kotler, M. (2005). Topiramate versus fluvoxamine in the treatment of pathological gambling: a randomized, blind-rater comparison study. *Clinical neuropharmacology*. 28(1):6-10.

Dannon, P. N., Lowengrub, K., Gonopolski, Y., Musin, E., Kotler, M. (2006). Pathological gambling: a review of phenomenological models and treatment modalities for an under recognized psychiatric disorder. *Primary Care Companion to the Journal of Clinical Psychiatry*. 8(6):334.

Diskin, K.M. & Hodgins, D. C. (2009). A randomized controlled trial of a single session motivational intervention for concerned gamblers. *Behaviour Research and Therapy*. 47(5):382-8.

Dowling, N., Smith, D., Thomas, T. (2007). A comparison of individual and group cognitive-behavioural treatment for female pathological gambling. *Behaviour Research and Therapy*, 45(9):2192-202.

Fong, T., Kalechstein, A., Bernhard, B., Rosenthal, R., Rugle, L. (2008). A double-blind, placebo-controlled trial of olanzapine for the treatment of video poker pathological gamblers. *Pharmacology Biochemistry and Behaviour*, 89(3):298-303.

Gay, A., Boutet, C., Sigaud, T., Kamgoue, A., Sevos, J., Brunelin, J. et al. (2017). A single session of repetitive transcranial magnetic stimulation of the prefrontal cortex reduces cue-induced craving in patients with gambling disorder. *European Psychiatry*. 41:68-74.

Grant, J. E., Kim, S. W., Potenza, M. N., Blanco, C., Ibanez, A., Stevens, L. et al. (2003). Paroxetine treatment of pathological gambling: a multi-centre randomized controlled trial. *International Clinical Psychopharmacology*. 18(4):243-9.

Grant, J. E., Potenza, M. N., Hollander, E., Cunningham-Williams, R., Nurminen, T., Smits, G. et al. (2006). Multicentre investigation of the opioid antagonist nalmefene in the treatment of pathological gambling. *American Journal of Psychiatry*. 163(2):303-12.

Grant, J. E., Kim, S. W., Odlaug, B. L. (2007). N-acetyl cysteine, a glutamate modulating agent, in the treatment of pathological gambling: a pilot study. *Biological Psychiatry*. 62(6): 652-7.

Grant, J. E. & Potenza, M. N. (2006). Escitalopram treatment of pathological gambling with co-occurring anxiety: an open-label pilot study with double-blind discontinuation. *International Clinical Psychopharmacology*, 21(4):203-9.
Grant, J. E., Kim, S. W., Hartman, B. K. (2008). A double-blind, placebo-controlled study of the opiate antagonist naltrexone in the treatment of pathological gambling urges. *Journal of Clinical Psychiatry*, 69(5):783-9.
Grant, J. E., Donahue, C. B., Odlaug, B. L., Kim, S. W., Miller, M. J., Petry, N. M. (2009). Imaginal desensitisation plus motivational interviewing for pathological gambling: randomised controlled trial. *British Journal of Psychiatry*, 195(3):266-7.
Grant, J. E., Chamberlain, S. R., Odlaug, B. L., Potenza, M. N., Kim, S. W. (2010). Memantine shows promise in reducing gambling severity and cognitive inflexibility in pathological gambling: a pilot study. *Psychopharmacology*, 212(4):603-12.
Grant, J. E., Odlaug, B. L., Potenza, M. N., Hollander, E., Kim, S. W. (2010). Nalmefene in the treatment of pathological gambling: multicentre, double-blind, placebo controlled study. *British Journal of Psychiatry*, 197(4):330-1.
Grant, J. E., Odlaug, B. L., Chamberlain, S. R., Potenza, M. N., Schreiber, L. R., Donahue, C. B. et al. (2014). A randomized, placebo-controlled trial of N acetyl cysteine plus imaginal desensitization for nicotine-dependent pathological gamblers. *Journal of Clinical Psychiatry*, 75(1):39-45.
Hollander, E., DeCaria, C. M., Finkell, J. N., Begaz, T., Wong, C. M., Cartwright, C. (2000). A randomized double-blind fluvoxamine/placebo crossover trial in pathologic gambling. *Biological Psychiatry*, 47(9):813-7.
Hollander, E., Pallanti, S., Allen, A., Sood, E., Rossi, N. B. (2005). Does sustained release lithium reduce impulsive gambling and affective instability versus placebo in pathological gamblers with bipolar spectrum disorders? *American Journal of Psychiatry*, 162(1):137-45.
Kim, S. W., Grant, J. E., Adson, D. E., Shin, Y. C. (2001). Double-blind naltrexone and placebo comparison study in the treatment of pathological gambling. *Biological Psychiatry*, 49(11):914-21.
Kim, S. W., Grant, J. E., Adson, D. E., Shin, Y. C., Zaninelli, R. (2002). A double-blind placebo-controlled study of the efficacy and safety of paroxetine in the treatment of pathological gambling. *Journal of Clinical Psychiatry*, 63(6):501-7.
Kovanen, L., Basnet, S., Castren, S., Pankakoski, M., Saarikoski, S. T., Partonen, T. et al. (2015). A randomised, double-blind, placebo-controlled trial of as needed naltrexone in the treatment of pathological gambling. *European Addiction Research*, 22(2):70-9.
Ladouceur, R., Sylvain, C., Boutin, C., Lachance, S., Doucet, C., Leblond, J. et al. (2001). Cognitive treatment of pathological gambling. *Journal of Nervous and Mental Disease*, 189(11):774-80.
Ladouceur, R., Sylvain, C., Boutin, C., Lachance, S., Doucet, C., Leblond, J. (2003). Group therapy for pathological gamblers: A cognitive approach. *Behaviour Research and Therapy*, 41(5):587-96.
Marceaux, J. C. & Melville, C. L. (2011). Twelve-step facilitated versus mapping enhanced cognitive-behavioural therapy for pathological gambling: A controlled study. *Journal of Gambling Studies*, 27(1):171-90.
Melville, C. L., Davis, C. S., Matzenbacher, D. L., Clayborne, J. (2004). Node-link mapping-enhanced group treatment for pathological gambling. *Addictive Behaviours*, 29(1):73-87.
McElroy, S. L., Nelson, E. B., Welge, J. A., Kaehler, L., Keck Jr, P. E. (2008). Olanzapine in the, Treatment of Pathological Gambling: A Negative Randomized Placebo Controlled Trial.

Journal of Clinical Psychiatry, 69(3):433-40.
Milosevic, A. & Ledgerwood, D. M. (2010). The subtyping of pathological gambling: A comprehensive review. *Clinical Psychology Review*, 30(8):988-98.
Oei, T. P., Raylu, N., Casey, L. M. (2010). Effectiveness of group and individual formats of a combined motivational interviewing and cognitive behavioural treatment program for problem gambling: a randomized controlled trial. *Behavioural and Cognitive Psychotherapy*, 38(02):233-8.
Petry, N. M., Ammerman, Y., Bohl, J., Doersch, A., Gay, H., Kadden, R. et al. (2006). Cognitive-behavioural therapy for pathological gamblers. *Journal of Consulting and Clinical Psychology*, 74(3):555.
Petry, N. M., Weinstock, J., Ledgerwood, D. M., Morasco, B. (2008). A randomized trial of brief interventions for problem and pathological gamblers. *Journal of Consulting and Clinical Psychology*, 76(2):318.
Petry, N. M., Weinstock, J., Morasco, B. J., Ledgerwood, D. M. (2009). Brief motivational interventions for college student problem gamblers. *Addiction*, 104(9):1569-78.
Saiz-Ruiz, J., Blanco, C., Ibáñez, A., Masramon, X., Gómez, M. M., Madrigal, M. et al. (2005). Sertraline treatment of pathological gambling: a pilot study. *Journal of Clinical Psychiatry*, 66(1):28-33.
Slutske, W. S. (2006). Natural recovery and treatment-seeking in pathological gambling: Results of two US national surveys. *American Journal of Psychiatry*, 163(2):297-302.
Suurvali, H., Hodgins, D. C., Cunningham, J. A. (2010). Motivators for resolving or seeking help for gambling problems: A review of the empirical literature. *Journal of Gambling Studies*, 26(1):1-33.
Sylvain, C., Ladouceur, R., Boisvert, J. M. (1997). Cognitive and behavioural treatment of pathological gambling: A controlled study. *Journal of Consulting and Clinical Psychology*, 65(5):727.
Thomas, A., Bonanni, L., Gambi, F., Di Iorio, A., Onofrj, M. (2010). Pathological gambling in Parkinson disease is reduced by amantadine. *Annals of Neurology*, 68(3):400-4.
Toneatto, T., Brands, B., Selby, P. (2009). A Randomized, Double Blind, Placebo Controlled Trial of Naltrexone in the Treatment of Concurrent Alcohol Use Disorder and Pathological Gambling. *American Journal of Addictions*, 18(3):219-25.

Chapter 9

Working with families of gamblers in India

Richard Velleman

Why families are important in the area of gambling problems

Our recent review of the impact of gambling in India (George, Velleman & Nadkarni, 2017), concluded that there was a paucity of research which had been conducted on gambling in India. We found only three studies of gambling from India: a survey of psychiatrists, looking at their 'exposure' to gamblers in their practice, their attitudes towards gamblers and their awareness of problem gambling; a study of college students' gambling habits; and a study of school students' gambling behaviours.

Nevertheless, we concluded that there was a great deal which we in India could learn from the research which had been undertaken in other countries. From that research, we knew that "*Problem gambling is associated with a range of health and social harms and adversely affects the individual, the family and society . It can negatively impact the gambler's physical (Morasco et al, 2006) health and gamblers tend to have high rates of various psychosomatic symptoms (cardiovascular, musculoskeletal, gastrointestinal and other non-specific psychosomatic symptoms) and mental health problems such as depression, anxiety, substance misuse and personality disorders (Petry et al, 2005). Problem gambling has a significant impact on the individual's financial situation, often resulting in large debts, poverty and even bankruptcy. It is also associated with criminal activities, ranging from theft and prostitution to violent crime, with obvious legal consequences.* "

It is obvious that this range of problems, affecting this range of elements (the gamblers physical and mental health, the family's finances, and the resulting criminal and legal effects), will all have strongly negative impacts on family members. Alongside that, problem gambling can adversely affect a gambler's interpersonal relationships with family members, resulting in relationship problems, neglect of the family, and sometimes leading to problems such as domestic violence and abuse (Mullean et al, 2002; Verma & Collumbien, 2003) aimed at both adults in the family and children.

This view that this range of problems will have major negative consequences on family members is backed-up by the worldwide international literature on the effects of addiction on families (whether the addiction is problematic gambling, or alcohol misuse, or drug misuse) (Kalischuk et al, 2006; Orford et al, 2013; Velleman, 2004). This literature shows that families are badly affected when a close relative develops a problem with gambling or any other addiction. On the one hand, the family as a whole - the structure and functioning of the family as a system of relationships - is disturbed, often severely: rituals, roles, routines, communication patterns, social life, finances: all are often severely impacted (Kourgiantakis et al, 2013; Velleman, 2004). Although research in this area within India is sparse, what little there is corroborates these more general findings:

Rituals: A substantial part of family life consists of rituals in the sense of repeated gatherings and set modes of behaviour which define the occasion or the day as being special, different from other days and occasions, and especially important precisely in the sense of being designed or expected to cement family relationships (Mullatti, 1995; Thomas & Bhugra, 2014). Examples are birthdays, anniversaries, religious observations, and a host of other ways in which one family and the way it comports itself differ from another family. One of the prime consequences of gambling and other addiction problems is that it is highly disruptive of family rituals (Bennett & Wolin, 1990; Mullatti, 1995; Murthy, 2015; Wolin et al, 1980).

Roles: Gambling and other addiction problems also tend to change the roles played by family members in relation to one another and the outside world (Kalischuk et al, 2006; Orford et al, 2013; Velleman et al, 2015). As one family member develops a gambling problem, the others gradually and of necessity take over his or her role. Eventually, one member may be performing all the family roles - finances, disciplining, and shopping, cleaning, and household management.

Routines: Another likely consequence of problem gambling is that behaviour becomes unpredictable, and this makes it very difficult for the family to plan or commit to routines (Finanet et al, 2015; Kuntscheet et al, 2006; McArdle et al, 2002). Will (s) he be able to collect the child from school? When will

(s) he come home, and in what state? Should meals be served or not? This constant uncertainty can be highly disruptive and it helps to explain a commonly found paradox in such families: that while the problem gambler may be doing little in the family, he or she nonetheless appears to dominate life.

Communication: Gambling problems affect communications between family members (Elgar, Craig and Trites, 2013; Masood and Sahar, 2014). The person with the problem may refuse to talk about it; or alternatively, the gambling and the often accompanying alcohol or other substance use may 'loosen the tongue' and things might be said which would otherwise not have been, thereby increasing marital and family conflict. Communication about (or in the midst of) a gambling problem not only changes the emotional quality of communication - discussions turning into rows and recriminations; the gambling and its effects also may grow to dominate the content of communication.

Social Life: Most people find it extraordinarily difficult to explain to friends and neighbours that a relative has a gambling problem. The social embarrassment, and the unpredictability associated with gambling problems, make it awkward to invite others into the family home, or accept invitations, or attend social gatherings. The family tends to become increasingly socially isolated (Orford et al, 2005; Orford et al, 1998).

Finances: Financial problems are always a further major strain for the family when there are addiction problems, but with gambling, this aspect is even further exacerbated (Chan, Dowling, Jackson & Shek, 2016; Dowling, Rodda, Lubman & Jackson, 2014; Mathews & Volberg, 2013). Money *spent* on gambling is not available for other family expenditures and gambling problems result in the family's *income* being greatly diminished. Jobs are lost, the rent is not paid, debts accumulate, accommodation is lost, and power is cut off.

As well as these problems in family structure and functioning, the range of issues outlined above in relation to a relative's gambling problems (the relative's physical and mental health problems, the financial and legal problems, etc.) often lead to the affected family members also demonstrating high levels of problem (Kourgiantakis et al, 2013; Patford, 2009; Velleman et al, 2015). These are world-wide phenomena, essentially similar in various cultures (Orford et al, 2005, 2013), so it is not surprising that this range of family and individual problems occur in India as well.

Among the most serious of the problems for affected family members associated with a relative's gambling is violence. It has been shown in both the International literature and in the small amount of research undertaken in India that there is a major relationship between gambling (and also alcohol misuse) and all aspects of domestic violence, including both spouse-to-spouse violence and child abuse (International: Afifi et al, 2010; Black et al, 2012; Korman et al, 2008; Kourgiantakis et al, 2013; Suomi et al, 2013; Indian: Ackerson and Subramanian, 2008; Das et al, 2013; Fernandes, 1997; Kombarakaran, 2004; Martin et al, 1999a,b; Panda & Agarwal, 2005; Rao, 1997; Srinivasan & Bedi, 2007; Stone & James, 1995; Verma & Collumbien, 2003). Internationally, a number of studies have shown a link between intimate partner violence and problem gambling (Afifi et al, 2010; Korman et al, 2008), as well as childhood maltreatment and problem gambling (Afifi et al, 2010; Black et al, 2012). Importantly, in India this relationship between gambling, alcohol use and domestic violence is especially disturbing. Although as mentioned above there has been very little research within the whole area of gambling in India, even with this paucity of research the relationship with domestic violence is remarkably strong. So for example, Verma & Collumbien, 2003 showed, in their community based research project which examined a large slum community in the north-eastern part of Mumbai consisting of about 100,000 inhabitants, using both in-depth qualitative work, followed by two surveys, one of 1,279 currently married men, another of 553 currently married women, that gambling was very highly statistically significantly linked to wife-beating in past year, both directly ($p<0.0001$) and as part of the logistic regression (showing that gambling was strongly associated with physical abuse in the last year (OR=2.15)). These authors concluded that "*In India, wife beating is closely linked with other less-acceptable behaviours on the part of men like gambling, alcohol consumption and extra-marital and pr emarital sex*".

The issue of domestic violence is further exacerbated by the co-relationship with alcohol misuse: at least 14% of alcohol or other drugs misusers also have serious co-morbid 'pathological' gambling problems, with around 23% suffering conditions along the broader spectrum of problem gambling (Cowlishaw, Merkouris, Chapman & Radermacher, 2014); and in India, Rao (1997) showed that "*Abuse is more likely when ... husbands ar e alcoholic, and when the cause of the abuse is per ceived as "legitimate" by the community. Survey data ... confirm that the risk of wife abuse significantly increases with ... alcohol consumption* "; and Srinivasan &

Bedi (2007) reported that "*A number of women pointed out the link between alcohol and violence. In response to questions on the reasons for violence, several respondents mentioned that their husbands resort to violence when they are drunk. In group discussions several factors such as economic and social stress, peer pressure, and the availability of liquor were cited as reasons for drunkenness. ... It is likely that the same observed and unobserved factors that create economic and social stress and lead a man to inflict violence are likely to drive excessive alcohol consumption. This suggests that drunkenness should not be treated as an exogenous variable but as an outcome of the same factors that may drive a man's violent actions*".

Effects on children: Living as a child with a parent with a gambling problem is also highly problematic (Kourgiantakis et al, 2013; Velleman et al, 2015). First, the fact that domestic violence is highly prevalent within families where someone has a gambling problem has major ramification for children in those families: it is the case that domestic violence is one of the prime factors associated with all risks to children and to their subsequent development (Velleman & Orford, 1999; Velleman & Templeton, 2007, 2016). Second, even if violence is not part of the child's experience, the disruption and disharmony associated with a parent having a gambling problem, and the resulting impacts on parental and family relationships, lead to many major negative consequences (Darbyshire et al, 2001a, b; Kalischuk, 2010; Vitaro et al, 2008). The effects of parental gambling problem on children are often long-standing, stretching into mid-adolescence, early adulthood, and beyond, with both higher rates of depression and of conduct problems (Vitaro et al, 2008).

Velleman et al (2015) recently reviewed the International evidence on the effects on family members if a close relative had a gambling problem. That review concluded that "*There is no doubt that gambling problems cause major difficulties for family members, (with) major impacts that such problems have both on adult family members and on children. ... There are strong similarities with the effects that other addictive problems (such as alcohol and drug problems) have on families, and some suggestion that problems in some areas may be even worse for families of those with gambling problems, due to the even more hidden nature of gambling disorders and the general ignorance on the part of the general public as to the existence of such problems. Also not in doubt is the conclusion that adult and child family members require help with the difficulties they face. It is vital that major treatment and prevention initiatives are undertaken to help deal with this great and growing problem.*"

The George et al (2017) review also concluded that "*Treatment/support should also be offered to carers of gamblers such as family and close friends: there are structured, evidence-based treatments for those affected by someone else's gambling (George and Bowden-Jones, 2015) and Gamblers Anonymous also runs support groups for families and friends called Gam-Anon.*" The next section in this chapter will examine various models of working with families of gamblers.

Working with families of gamblers internationally

The amount of help which is provided to family members affected by someone with a gambling problem is related to the availability of help accessible for the problem gamblers – if provision for gamblers is low, then the provision for affected family members will be even lower. Internationally, research shows that only 3%-6% of individuals with gambling problems seek treatment (Suurvali, Hodgins, Toneatto & Cunningham, 2008), and there is a high rate of attrition while in treatment: Ladouceur, Gosselin, Laberge, & Blaszczynski, 2001 found that of those who seek treatment, only 50% remain in treatment until its completion. Gambling individuals also have a high risk of relapse, with Hodgins & el-Guebaly, 2004 reporting from their longitudinal study that only 8% of gambling individuals remained abstinent after 1 year. It is against that backdrop that provision of help for affected family members must be examined.

A number of family focused interventions have been developed over the years in the gambling and substance misuse fields. These tend to fall into three broad areas (Copello, Velleman & Templeton, 2005), although there is some level of overlap:

- working with family members to promote the entry and engagement of misusers into treatment,
- joint involvement of family members and misusing relatives in the treatment of the misuser,
- and interventions responding to the needs of the family members in their own right.

As with many other areas, the vast majority of the research into family-focussed work has been undertaken in the substance misuse field (either alcohol or drugs) with far less being undertaken in the gambling field. Nevertheless, due to huge similarities between problem gambling, problem drug use, and problem alcohol use, these will be summarised together below.

In terms of first area (working with family members to promote the entry and engagement of misusers into treatment), there is robust evidence that working with family members affected by gambling (Hodgins, Shead, & Makarchuk, 2007; Makarchuk et al, 2002; Nayoski & Hodgins, 2016;Peden, 2011; Rychtarik & McGillicuddy, 2006) or substance misuse (Bischof, Iwen, Freyer-Adam & Rumpf, 2016; Brigham, Slesnick, Winhusen, et al, 2014; Roozen et al, 2009, 2010) can trigger treatment entry for the relative with the problem, although the rate of problem gamblers entering treatment is generally quite small (for example, only about 17% of gambling individuals entered treatment by the 6-month follow-up, following these interventions. This can appear small, but without these interventions, the rates for those with gambling problems entering treatment are 3%-6%, as reported above). These findings are evident when working with all of gambling, alcohol and drug problems (Roozen et al, 2010), although more studies have been reported with alcohol related problems (Roozen et al, 2009), and with some approaches having more robust evaluations (e.g. CRAFT: Meyers et al, 2011; Roozen et al, 2009) than do others. In a number of studies, it has also been reported that even if the substance misuser does not enter treatment, outcomes for family members can still be positive (e.g. Hodgins, Shead & Makarchuk, 2007; Hodgins, Toneatto, Makarchuk, Skinner, & Vincent, 2007; Makarchuk et al, 2002; Peden, 2011; Rychtarik & McGillicuddy, 2006 – all of these used the CRAFT intervention as the basis for their work), provided the treatments have elements built into them to address family member's stress and psychological well-being.

In terms of the second area (joint involvement of family members and misusing relatives in the treatment of the misuser), there is also evidence that family involvement in treatment can be very effective (Ingle et al, 2008; Kourgiantakis et al, 2013). Although the evidence could be strengthened, what evidence has been published suggests that many interventions reviewed are promising and should not be excluded from further evaluation and development. Some approaches have more robust evaluation (e.g.

Behavioural Couples Therapy, Kourgiantakis et al, 2013; Lee, 2002; Lee & Rovers, 2008), but family therapy approaches have also shown good outcomes with particular emphasis on the misuser's gambling, alcohol or drug consumption (Liddle, 2004; Mittal and Hardy, 2005; Tanner-Smith et al, 2013). Network methods show some promise (e.g. Copello, Orford, Hogson & Tober, 2009; Galanter, 1999; Williamson, Smith, Orford et al, 2007) although further rigorous evaluation is required. One advantage of such methods is that other people who are concerned about someone's drinking or drug use can also be involved in treatment even if that person is not a family member (e.g. neighbours, work colleagues, friends).

In terms of the third area, of interventions that try to alleviate the problems caused to family members by the gambling or substance misuse of a relative, there is growing evidence that such interventions are very helpful to family members particularly in terms of reductions in symptoms of stress and ill-health present in family members (Copello, Templeton, Orford & Velleman, 2010; Hodgins, Shead, & Makarchuk, 2007; Hodgins, Toneatto, Makarchuk, Skinner, & Vincent, 2007; Makarchuk et al, 2002; Peden, 2011; Rychtarik & McGillicuddy, 2006; Velleman et al, 2008; Velleman, Orford, Templeton, et al, 2011). A number of studies have shown that, even though the gambling or substance misusing relative was not involved in the study and was not receiving any treatment for problem gambling or substance misuse, the affected family member showed decreased levels of personal distress and increases in relationship satisfaction.

There are also a slowly growing number of studies which have looked especially at the needs of children if one or both parents has a gambling or substance misuse problem (Darbyshire et al, 2001a,b; Velleman & Templeton, 2007, 2016; Vitaro et al, 2008), showing that these children frequently develop major emotional and behavioural problems as a result of living in such situations, and that they are at greater risk of developing gambling, substance misuse and other problems in turn when they reach adolescence and adulthood. However, in a similar way as with affected adults, few services and few interventions have been developed to assist these children who are having to cope with a relative's (usually a parent's) drinking or drug taking, either in dealing with their current distress or in trying to prevent future problems (Chan et al, 2016;Forrester, Holland, Williams et al, 2014; Forrester & Harwin, 2011; Kroll & Taylor, 2003; Neger & Prinz, 2015; Orford et al, 2013; Rahman et al, 2014; Rane et al, 2017; Taylor & Kroll, 2004).

Working with families of gamblers in India

There is virtually no treatment available in India for people with gambling problems, never mind their families. Benegal (2013) reported that when his survey of members of the Indian Psychiatric Society "*revealed that such clients were rarely encountered in clinical psychiatric practice*" (p 2065); that only four meetings of Gamblers Anonymous are listed in the Gamblers Anonymous International directory across all of India, all of them in large metropolitan cities; and that an internet search to identify "identify published and unpublished studies on problem/ pathological gambling in India" produced no reports or trials of treatment for problem gambling. This lack of treatment provision for problem gamblers in India mirrors the situation internationally, although it is worse in India.

There are some treatment facilities in India, of course, although generally mental health services in India are extremely limited (Gururaj et al, 2016; Patel et al, 2017). Nevertheless, some practitioners in India utilise evidence-based therapeutic methods. For example, Mittal and Hardy (2005) reviewed the current status and future of family therapy in India, concluding that "*there is discernible family therapy activity thr oughout India. In fact, the practice of marriage and family counselling has existed in India for quite some time although it has not been r egarded as a formalized profession.*" (p 298).

Against this backdrop of an almost total lack of treatment availability for problem gamblers, it is not surprising to find that there exist no services, to this author's knowledge, offering help to affected family members of those with gambling problems.

Challenges to working with families of gamblers in India

There are many challenges to working with families of gamblers in India.

First, there is still debate in India over whether problem gambling even exists as an addictive disorder needing treatment (Prakash et al, 2012). If problem gambling is not recognised as an issue where people need help or treatment, then obtaining help or treatment for their affected family members will be even more problematic.

Second, if society in general and helping professionals in particular do not see problem gambling as requiring treatment, it is likely that the affected family members will themselves not conceptualise it in this way. It is much more likely that affected family members will simply see such problems as their 'fate', something with which they simply have to 'put up with' (Murthy, 2015).

Third, this links with the larger area of treatment and help for those affected by domestic violence – both focused on adults such as spousal and parental abuse, and focused on children, in terms of physical and sexual abuse. There is a massive and under-acknowledged problem with all forms of domestic abuse within India (Ackerson and Subramanian, 2008; Das et al, 2013; Fernandes, 1997; Kombarakaran, 2004; Martin et al, 1999a, b; Panda & Agarwal, 2005; Rao, 1997; Srinivasan & Bedi, 2007; Stone and James, 1995), which has contributed to the vast treatment gap between those subjected to such abuse and the provision of any help for them. Given the links between problem gambling, alcohol misuse, and domestic violence, this treatment gap makes the chances of family members affected by a relative's gambling problem receiving help or treatment even less likely.

Fourth, gambling itself is not a high priority policy are for Indian national and state governments (Benegal, 2013), so attempting to place the needs of affected family members on that agenda face considerable difficulties.

Conclusions

Given the paucity of research on gambling in India, it is not surprising that there has been almost no research undertaken on the impact on families, and none on treatments for these families, either as a whole or for individual affected family members.

Nevertheless, certain conclusions can be reached:

- Problem gambling has major negative consequences on family members.
- The structure and functioning of the family as a system of relationships is disturbed, often severely.
- Individual family members suffer a range of psychological and physical problems due to the stresses they bear.
- Among the most serious of the problems for affected family members associated with a relative's gambling is violence: there is a major relationship between gambling and all aspects of domestic violence, including both spouse-to-spouse violence and child abuse.
- Living as a child with a parent with a gambling problem is also highly problematic, with the effects often being long-standing, stretching into mid-adolescence, early adulthood, and beyond.

- There is very little treatment available for problem gamblers, and even less for their affected family members.
- What research there has been into help for affected family members has tended to look at three broad areas: working with family members to promote the entry and engagement of gamblers into treatment; joint involvement of family members and relatives in the treatment of the gambler; and interventions responding to the needs of the family members in their own right.
- There is evidence from both the few studies on family members of problem gamblers, and the more numerous studies of family members whose relatives have other addiction problems such as alcohol or drug problems, that work with or including affected family members produces positive results.
- There are, however, many significant challenges in developing better services for family members affected by their relative's problem gambling, concerning recognition of the problem in the first place, dealing with the often accompanying violence and alcohol misuse, and raising the status of problem gambling and its effects on families in policy circles, so that more effective national and state policies related to gambling are developed and introduced.

The most important conclusion, of course, is that much more work needs to be undertaken: at the moment, huge numbers of people across India are suffering as affected family members of people with gambling problems, and they are receiving no help. It is vital that more research is undertaken to clarify the impact on these affected family members here in India, to develop culturally appropriate interventions to help these affected family members, and to generate policy initiatives so that gambling difficulties, and the problems that these cause for family members, are accorded the importance and priority that they deserve.

Key points

- Gambling disorder has major negative consequences on family members. The structure and functioning of the family as a system of relationships is disturbed, often severely.
- Individual family members suffer a range of psychological and physical problems due to the stresses they bear. There is a major relationship between gambling and all aspects of domestic violence, including both spouse-to-spouse violence and child abuse.
- There is very little treatment available for problem gamblers in India, and even less for their affected family members.
- What research there has been into help for affected family members has tended to look at

three broad areas: working with family members to promote the entry and engagement of gamblers into treatment; joint involvement of family members and relatives in the treatment of the gambler; and interventions responding to the needs of the family members in their own right.
- There is evidence from both the few studies on family members of problem gamblers, and the more numerous studies of family members whose relatives have other addiction problems such as alcohol or drug problems, that work with or including affected family members produces positive results.
- There are significant challenges to working with families of gamblers in India, including: recognition of the problem, dealing with the often accompanying violence and alcohol misuse, and raising the status of problem gambling and its effects on families in policy circles.

References

Ackerson, L. & Subramanian, S. (2008). Domestic violence and chronic malnutrition among women and children in India. *American Journal of Epidemiology*, 167(10), 1188–1196.

Afifi, T. O., Brownridge, D. A., MacMillan, H. & Sareen, J. (2010). The relationship of gambling to intimate partner violence and child maltreatment in a nationally representative sample. *Journal of Psychiatric Research*, *44*, 331–337.

Benegal, V. (2013). Gambling experiences, problems and policy in India: a historical analysis. *Addiction*, 108, 2062–2067.

Bennett, L. & Wolin, S. (1990) Family culture and alcoholism transmission. In Collins, R., Leonard, K. and Searles, J. (Eds.) *Alcohol and the family: research & clinical perspectives* New York; Guilford Press.

Bischof, G., Iwen, J., Freyer-Adam, J., Rumpf, H. (2016). Efficacy of the Community Reinforcement and Family Training for concerned significant others of treatment-refusing individuals with alcohol dependence - A randomized controlled trial. *Drug and Alcohol Dependence*, 163, 179-185.

Black, D., Shaw, M., McCormick, B., Allen, J. (2012). Marital status, childhood maltreatment, and family dysfunction: A controlled study of pathological gambling. *Journal of Clinical Psychiatry*, *73*, 1293–1297.

Brigham, G., Slesnick, N., Winhusen, T., Lewis, D., Guo, X., Somoza, E. (2014). A randomized pilot clinical trial to evaluate the efficacy of Community Reinforcement and Family Training for Treatment Retention (CRAFT-T) for improving outcomes for patients completing opioid detoxification. *Drug and Alcohol Dependence*, 138, 240-243.

Chan, E., Dowling, N., Jackson A., Shek, D. (2016). Gambling related family coping and the impact of problem gambling on families in Hong Kong. *Asian Journal of Gambling Issues and Public Health*, 6(1)

Copello, A., Orford, J., Hogson. R., Tober, G. (2009). *Social Behaviour and Network Therapy for Alcohol Problems*. London: Routledge.

Copello, A., Templeton, L., Orford, J., Velleman, R. (2010). The 5-Step Method: evidence of gains for affected family members. *Drugs: Education, Prevention and Policy*, 17 (Supplement 1), 100–112.

Copello, A., Velleman, R., Templeton, L. (2005). Family interventions in the treatment of alcohol and drug problems. *Drug & Alcohol Review*, 24(4), 369-385.

Cowlishaw, S., Merkouris, S., Chapman, A., Radermacher, H. (2014). Pathological and problem gambling in substance use treatment: A systematic review and meta-analysis. *Journal of Substance Abuse Treatment*, 46(2), 98-105.

Darbyshire, P., Oster, C., Carrig, H. (2001a). The experience of pervasive loss: Children and young people living in a family where parental gambling is a problem. *Journal of Gambling Studies, 17*, 23–45.

Darbyshire, P., Oster, C., Carrig, H. (2001b). Children of parent(s) who have a gambling problem: a review of the literature and commentary on research approaches. *Health and Social Care in the Community*. 9, 185-193.

Das, S., Bapat, U., More, N., Alcock, G., Joshi, W., Pantvaidya, S. et al. (2013). Intimate partner violence against women during and after pregnancy - a cross-sectional study in Mumbai slums. *BMC Public Health*, 13, 817, 1-12.

Dowling, N., Rodda, S., Lubman, D., Jackson, A. (2014). The impacts of problem gambling on concerned significant others accessing web-based counselling. *Addictive Behaviours*, 39(8), 1253-1257.

Elgar, F., Craig, W., Trites, S. (2013). Family dinners, communication, and mental health in Canadian adolescents. *Journal of Adolescent Health*, 52 (4), 433-438.

Fernandes, L. (1997). Beyond public spaces and private spheres - gender, family, and working-class politics in India. *Feminist Studies*, 23(3), 525-547.

Finan, L., Schulz, J., Gordon, M., Ohannessian, C. (2015). Parental problem drinking and adolescent externalizing behaviours: The mediating role of family functioning. *Journal of Adolescence*, 43, 100-110.

Forrester, D., Holland, S., Williams, A., Copello, A. (2014). Helping families where parents misuse drugs or alcohol? A mixed methods comparative evaluation of an intensive family preservation service. *Child and Family Social Work*, 21 (1), 65–75.

Forrester, D. & Harwin, J. (2011). *Parental Misuse of Drugs and Alcohol: Effective Intervention and Assessment*. Chichester; Wiley.

Galanter, M. (1999). *Network Therapy for Alcohol and Drug Abuse* (Expanded Edition). New York, NY: Guilford.

George, S. & Bowden-Jones, H. (2015). Family interventions in gambling. In: Bowden-Jones, H. and George, S. (Eds) *A Clinician's Guide to Working with Problem Gamblers*. London: Routledge & the Royal College of Psychiatrists.

George, S., Velleman, R., Nadkarni, A. (2017). Gambling in India: Past, present and future. *Asian Journal of Psychiatry*, 26, 39–43.

Gururaj, G., Varghese, M., Benegal, V., Rao, G. N., Pathak, K., Singh, L. K. et al. (2016). *National Mental Health Survey of India, 2015-16: Summary*. Bengaluru: National Institute of Mental Health and Neuro Sciences.

Hodgins, D. & el-Guebaly, N. (2004). Retrospective and prospective reports of precipitants to relapse in pathological gambling. *Journal of Consulting and Clinical Psychology*, *72*, 72–80.

Hodgins, D., Shead, N., Makarchuk, K. (2007). Relationship satisfaction and psychological distress among concerned significant others of pathological gamblers. *The Journal of Nervous and Mental Disease, 195*, 65–71.

Hodgins, D., Toneatto, T., Makarchuk, K., Skinner, W., Vincent, S. (2007). Minimal treatment approaches for concerned significant others of problem gamblers: A randomized control trial. *Journal of Gambling Studies, 23*, 215–230.

Ingle, P., Marotta, J., McMillan, G., Wisdom, J. P. (2008). Significant others and problem gambling treatment outcomes. *Journal of Gambling Studies, 24*, 381–392.

Kalischuk, R., Nowatzki, N., Cardwell, K., Klein, K., Solowoniuk, J. (2006). Problem Gambling and its Impact on Families: A Literature Review. *International Gambling Studies*, 6 (1), 31-60.
Kalischuk, R. (2010). Co - creating Life Pathways: Problem Gambling and its Impact on Families. *The Family Journal*, 18(1), 7-17.
Kombarakaran, F. (2004). Street children of Bombay - their stresses and strategies of coping. *Children and Youth Services Review*, 26, 853-871.
Korman, L., Collins, J., Dutton, D., Dhayananthan, B., Littman-Sharp, N., Skinner, W. (2008). Problem gambling and intimate partner violence. *Journal of Gambling Studies, 24*, 13–23.
Kourgiantakis, T., Saint-Jacques, M., Tremblay, J. (2013). Problem gambling and families - a systematic review. *Journal of Social Work Practice in the Addictions*, 13 (4), 353-372.
Kroll, B. & Taylor, A. (2003). *Parental Substance Misuse and Child W elfare*. London; Jessica Kingsley Publishers.
Kuntsche, S., Gmel, G., Knibbe, R., Kuendigkim, H., Bloomfield, K., Kramer, S. et al. (2006). Gender and cultural differences in the association between family roles, social stratification, and alcohol use: a European cross-cultural analysis. *Alcohol and Alcoholism*, 41 (suppl 1), i37–i46.
Ladouceur, R., Gosselin, P., Laberge, M., Blaszczynski, A. (2001). Drop-outs in clinical research: Do results reported in the field of addiction reflect clinical reality? *The Behaviour Therapist, 24*, 44–46.
Lee, B. (2002). *Well-being by choice not by chance: An integrative system-based couple treatment model for problem gambling* (Final report). Guelph, Canada: Ontario Problem Gambling Research Centre.
Lee, B. & Rovers, M. (2008) Bringing torn lives together again: Effects of the first congruence couple therapy application to clients in pathological gambling. *International Gambling Studies, 8*, 113–129.
Liddle, H. (2004). Family-based therapies for adolescent alcohol and drug use: research contributions and future research needs. *Addiction*, 99 (s2), 76-92.
Makarchuk, K., Hodgins, D., Peden, N. (2002). Development of a brief intervention for concerned significant others of problem gamblers. *Addictive Disorders & Their Treatment, 1*, 126–134.
Martin, S., Kilgallen, Â. Tsui, A., Maitra, K., Singh, K., Kupper, L. (1999a). Sexual behaviours and reproductive health outcomes: associations with wife abuse in India. *Journal of the American Medical Association*, 282, 1967-72.
Martin, S., Tsui, A., Maitra, K., Marinshaw, R. (1999b). Domestic violence in northern India. *American Journal of Epidemiology*, 150(4), 417-426.
Masood, S. & Sahar, N. (2014). An exploratory research on the role of family in youth's drug addiction. *Health Psychology and Behavioural Medicine*, 2(1), 820-832
Mathews. M. & Volberg. R. (2013). Impact of problem gambling on financial, emotional and social well-being of Singaporean families. *International Gambling Studies*, 13(1), 127-140.
McArdle, P., Wiegersma, A., Gilvarry, E., Kolte, B., McCarthy, S., Fitzgerald, M. et al. (2002). European adolescent substance use: the roles of family structure, function and gender. *Addiction*, 97, 329–336.
Meyers, R., Roozen, H., Smith, J. (2011). The Community Reinforcement Approach: an update of the evidence. *Alcohol Research & Health*, 33 (4), 380-388.
Mittal, M. & Hardy, K. (2005). A re-examination of the current status and future of Family

Therapy in India. *Contemporary Family Therapy*, 27(3), 285-300.
Morasco, B., Pietrzak, R., Blanco, C., Grant, B., Hasin, D., Petry, N. (2006). Health problems and medical utilization associated with gambling disorders: Results from the National Epidemiologic Survey on alcohol and related conditions. *Psychosomatics*, 68, 976-984.
Mullatti, L. (1995). Families in India: Beliefs and Realities. *Journal of Comparative Family Studies*, 26 (1), 11-25.
Mullean, R., Denotter, T., Wadman, M., Tran, T., Anderson, J. (2002). Problem gambling in the partner of emergency department patient as a risk factor for intimate partner violence. *Journal of Emergency Medicine*, 23, 307–312.
Murthy, P. (2015). Culture and alcohol use in India. *World Cultural Psychiatry Research Review*, 10(1), 27-39.
Nayoski, N. & Hodgins, D. (2016). The efficacy of individual Community Reinforcement and Family Training (CRAFT) for concerned significant others of problem gamblers. *Journal of Gambling Issues*, 33, 189-212.
Neger, E. & Prinz, R. (2015). Interventions to address parenting and parental substance abuse: Conceptual and methodological considerations. *Clinical Psychology Review*, 39, 71-82.
Orford, J., Natera, G., Copello, A., Atkinson, C., Tiburcio, M., Velleman, R. et al. (2005). *Coping with Alcohol and Drug Problems: The Experiences of Family Members in Three Contrasting Cultures*. London; Routledge.
Orford, J., Natera, G., Davies, J., Nava, A., Mora, J., Rigby, K.et al. (1998). Social support in coping with alcohol and drug problems at home: findings from Mexican and English families. *Addiction Research*, 6(5), 395-420.
Orford, J., Velleman, R., Natera, G., Templeton, L., Copello, A. (2013). Addiction in the family is a major but neglected contributor to the global burden of adult ill-health. *Social Science and Medicine*, 78, 70-77.
Panda, P. & Agarwal, B. (2005). Marital violence, human development and women's property status in India. *World Development*, 33(5), 823–850.
Patel, V., Xiao, S., Chen, H., Hanna, F., Jotheeswaran, A. T., Luo, D. et al. (2017). The magnitude of and health system responses to the mental health treatment gap in adults in India and China. *The Lancet*, 388 (10063), 3074-84.
Patford, J. (2009). For worse, for poorer and in ill health - how women experience, understand and respond to a partner's gambling problems. *International Journal of Mental Health and Addiction*, 7(1), 177–189.
Peden, N. (2011). *The efficacy of individual community reinforcement and family training (CRAFT) with concerned significant others of problem gamblers* (Doctoral dissertation). Available from ProQuest Dissertations and Theses database (Accession No. NR81461).
Petry, N., Stinson, F., Grant, B. (2005). Comorbidity of DSM-IV pathological gambling and other psychiatric disorders: results from the National Epidemiologic Survey on Alcohol and Related Conditions. *Journal of Clinical Psychiatry*, 66, 564–574.
Prakash, O., Avasthi, A., Benegal, V. (2012). Should pathological gambling be considered an addictive disorder? *Asian Journal of Psychiatry*, 5 (3), 211–214.
Rahman, A., Balodis, I., Pilver, C., Leeman, R., Hoff, R., Steinberg, M. et al. (2014). Adolescent alcohol-drinking frequency and problem-gambling severity: adolescent perceptions regarding problem-gambling prevention and parental/adult behaviours and attitudes. *Substance Abuse*, 35, 426-434.

Rane, A., Church, S., Bhatia, U., Orford, J., Velleman, R., Nadkarni, A. (2017). Psychosocial interventions for addiction-affected families in Low and Middle Income Countries: a systematic review. *Addictive Behaviours*, 74, early online, May 2017.
Rao, V. (1997). Wife-beating in rural South India - a qualitative and econometric analysis. *Social Science and Medicine*, 44, 1169-80.
Roozen, H., Blaauw, E., Meyers, R. (2009). Advances in management of Alcohol Use Disorders and intimate partner violence: Community Reinforcement and Family Training. *Psychiatry, Psychology and Law*, 16 (1), S74-S80.
Roozen, H., De Waart, R., Van Der Kroft, P. (2010). Community reinforcement and family training: an effective option to engage treatment-resistant substance-abusing individuals in treatment. *Addiction*, 105 (10), 1729–1738.
Rychtarik, R. & McGillicuddy, N. (2006). Preliminary evaluation of a coping skills training program for those with a pathological-gambling partner. *Journal of Gambling Studies, 22*, 165–178.
Srinivasan, S. & Bedi, A. (2007). Domestic violence and dowry - evidence from a South Indian village. *World Development*, 35(5), 857-880.
Stone, L. & James, C. (1995). Dowry, bride-burning, and female power in India. *Women's Studies International Forum*, 18(2), 125-134.
Suomi, A., Jackson, A., Dowling, N., Lavis, T., Patford, J., Thomas, S. et al. (2013). Problem gambling and family violence: family member reports of prevalence, family impacts and family coping. *Asian Journal of Gambling Issues and Public Health*, 3, 13-28.
Suurvali, H., Hodgins, D., Toneatto, T., Cunningham, J. (2008). Treatment seeking among Ontario problem gamblers: Results of a population survey. *Psychiatric Services, 59*, 1343–1346.
Tanner-Smith E., Wilson S., Lipsey M. (2013). The comparative effectiveness of outpatient treatment for adolescent substance abuse - A meta-analysis. *Journal of Substance Abuse Treatment*, 44, 145–158.
Thomas, B. & Bhugra, D. (2014). Preparation for parenthood programme: Experiences from southern India. *International Review of Psychiatry*, 26(4)493-499.
Taylor, A. & Kroll, B. (2004). Working with parental substance misuse: Dilemmas for practice. *British Journal of Social Work*, 34(8), 1115–1132.
Velleman, R. (2004). Alcohol and drug problems: an overview of the impact on children and the implications for practice. In Gopfert, M., Webster, J. and Seeman, M. (Eds.) *Seriously Disturbed and Mentally Ill Parents and their Children, 2d Edition*. Cambridge; Cambridge University Press, Chapter 13, pp 185-202.
Velleman, R., Arcidiacono, C., Procentese, F., Copello, A., Sarnacchiaro, P. (2008). A 5-Step intervention to help family members in Italy who live with substance misusers. *Journal of Mental Health*, 17(6), 643-655.
Velleman, R., Cousins, J., Orford, J. (2015). The effects of gambling on the family. In Bowden-Jones, H. and George, S. (Eds) *A Clinician's Guide to Working with Problem Gamblers*. London: Routledge & the Royal College of Psychiatrists.
Velleman, R. & Orford, J. (1999). *Risk & Resilience: Adults who were the Children of Problem Drinkers*. London; Harwood.
Velleman, R., Orford, J., Templeton, L., Copello, A., Patel, A., Moore, L. et al. (2011). 12-month follow-up after brief interventions in primary care for family members affected by the substance misuse problem of a close relative. *Addiction Research and Theory*, 19(4), 362-374.

Velleman, R. & Templeton, L. (2007). Understanding and modifying the impact of parents' substance misuse on children. *Advances in Psychiatric Treatment*, 13, 79-89.
Velleman, R. & Templeton, L. (2016). Impact of parents' substance misuse on children: an update from 2007. *BJPsych Advances (Advances in Psychiatric Treatment)*, 22, 108–117.
Verma, R. & Collumbien, M. (2003). Wife beating and the link with poor sexual health and risk behaviour among men in urban slums in India. *Journal of Comparative Family Studies*, 34 (1) [Violence against women in the family (Winter 2003)], 61-74.
Vitaro, F., Wanner, B., Brendgen, M., Tremblay, R. (2008). Offspring of parents with gambling problems: Adjustment problems and explanatory mechanisms. *Journal of Gambling Studies, 24*, 535–553.
Williamson, E, Smith M, Orford J, Copello, A., Day, E. (2007). Social Behaviour and Network Therapy for drug problems: evidence of benefits and challenges, *Addictive Disorders & their Treatment*, 6(4), 167-179.
Wolin, S., Bennett, L., Noonan, D., Teitelbaum, M. (1980). Disrupted family rituals: a factor in the intergenerational transmission of alcoholism. *Journal of Studies on Alcohol*, 41, 199 214.

Chapter 10

Delivering effective interventions for addictive disorders in primary care in low resource settings

Abhijit Nadkarni

Treatment of gambling disorders in primary care

Less than 10% of the individuals with gambling disorders seek formal treatment for their problems, and the reasons for poor treatment seeking include desire to handle the problem on their own, shame, and denial (Slutske, Blaszczynski & Martin 2009; Cunningham, 2005). On such a background the two important pillars of providing care for individuals with gambling disorder are increasing public awareness and increasing access to treatment models aimed at promotion of recovery process for such individuals.

Several interventions for gambling disorders have been proposed and tested, some of which are dependent on delivery by specialists while others are suitable to be delivered in primary care. A range of psychosocial interventions based on behavioural, cognitive, cognitive-behavioural, and MI theoretical models have shown to be effective in the treatment of gambling disorders (Pallesen et al, 2005; Gooding & Tarrier, 2009; Carlbring et al, 2010). The evidence for the role of family therapy models in the treatment of gambling disorders is in the nascent stages but the limited available evidence shows promise. Such interventions include Community Reinforcement and Family Therapy (CRAFT) in which family members are trained to use behavioural principles to reinforce non-gambling behaviour in non-treatment seeking individuals with gambling disorders, and a coping skill group therapy model aimed at family members to improve their ability to self-manage feelings of depression and anxiety (Makarchuk et al, 2002; Hodgins et al, 2007). Finally, although the evidence on the pharmacological treatment of gambling disorders appears promising, especially in the case of opioid antagonists, further research is needed with large samples to examined whether there is differential benefit from various drugs and to establish who would benefit more from pharmacotherapy or psychotherapy (Hodgins et al, 2011). Despite the evidence base, sometimes limited, one of the biggest barriers to accessing these interventions is the need for highly trained specialists to deliver them.

Based on evidence from the alcohol use disorders field, the interventions that are best suited for delivery by non-specialists in primary care are brief interventions (Kaner et al, 2007). There is some evidence of effectiveness of brief treatments for non-treatment seeking individuals with gambling disorders. Examples of such evidence based brief treatments for gambling disorders include a telephone-based MI session with a mailed self-help cognitive behavioural therapy workbook (Hodgins et al, 2011, 2004, 2009), web based MI and CBT with telephone support by therapist in Sweden (Carlbring & Smit, 2008), and a 5-minute session of behavioural advice and four sessions of MET plus CBT in the USA (Petry et al, 2008). There is no reason to believe that such brief treatments would not be feasible to be delivered in primary care by non-specialists. However, the field of gambling disorders is in its infancy and more rigorous research needs to be conducted to further develop and test the implementation of treatment models using easily accessible platforms such as primary care.

Even in the absence of robust evidence based interventions for gambling disorders because of regular and long-term contact with patients, primary care providers are in a unique position to recognize patients with gambling disorders, to provide a menu of treatment options, if available, and monitor response to treatment in these patients. The first step would be to screen for those who are potentially at high risk e.g. those presenting with psychosomatic symptoms, depression, and anxiety-spectrum disorders (George & Gerada, 2011). Short, structured, and easy to use screening tools such the Lie/Bet Questionnaire (Johnson et al, 1997) or the Early Intervention Gambling Health Test (EIGHT) (Sullivan, 1999) could be effectively used to identify gambling disorders in high risk individuals. Once problem gambling is identified, primary care providers could do a detailed assessment of the gambling history, sensitively broach the topic of the possible existence of gambling problems, thoughtfully motivate the patient to seek treatment, refer to appropriate services, if available, and monitor progress (Sullivan, 1999). A working example of such a model is a first of its kind pilot project in Birmingham, UK which included opportunistic screening and brief intervention in primary care, and onward referral where indicated (George & Gerada, 2011). However, implementation of such a primary care led model will require enhanced training of primary care providers as some of the biggest barriers to delivering care for gambling disorders are lack of awareness, knowledge, education, and training (Rowan and Galasso, 2000).

Burden of mental, neurological, and substance use disorders

Mental, neurological, and substance use (MNS) disorders are a heterogeneous group of disorders that share several important characteristics, such as symptoms driven by some degree of brain dysfunction, role of social determinants in their development and progression, frequent co-occurence in the same individual, profound effect on families and wider society, strong association with stigma and discrimination, and a chronic or relapsing course (Patel et al, 2016).

MNS disorders are significant contributors to the world's disease burden. Over a relatively short period of twenty years (1990-2010) the absolute disability-adjusted life-years (DALYs) due to MNS disorders rose by 41%; and the proportion of global disease burden attributed to MNS disorders rose from 7·3% to 10·4%. Furthermore, MNS disorders are the leading cause of years lived with disability (YLDs) globally and DALYs from MNS disorders are highest during early-to-mid-adulthood, the most productive years of a person's lifespan (Whiteford et al, 2013). Although, the contribution of the relative proportion of DALYs from MNS disorders to overall disease burden is higher in developed regions than in developing regions, because of the larger population size in LMICs, absolute DALYs from MNS disorders are much higher in LMICs (Whiteford et al, 2013). Examining substance use in particular, in both developing and developed regions, alcohol, ranks along with tobacco, high blood pressure, and high cholesterol as the biggest risk factor to global burden of disease (Ezzati et al, 2002). Drug use disorders directly account for 0·8% of all-cause DALYs; an increase of 52% over 20 years (1990 to 2010) (Degenhardt et al, 2013). Finally, it is important to remember that beyond the direct disease burden of substance use disorders there are substantial social and economic consequences of these disorders, on the affected individuals and families as well as on wider communities and economies. For example, the economic costs attributable to alcohol use and alcohol use disorders alone are estimated to amount to the equivalent of

1·3–3·3% of gross domestic product (GDP) in high-income and middle-income countries, two-thirds of the losses being productivity losses (Rehm et al, 2009). One would expect such economic costs to have a greater impact in already poorly resourced low income countries.

Considering the epidemiological picture outlined above it is not surprising that the World Health Organization's (WHO) flagship Mental Health Gap Action Programme (mhGAP) recognizes alcohol use disorders and drug use disorders as priority conditions representing a large burden in terms of mortality, morbidity, or disability, and have high economic costs (WHO 2008; 2004).

Evidence - based packages of care for substance use disorders

There exist a range of medications, psychological, and social interventions which can be used to attenuate the severity and course of MNS disorders, including substance use disorders. Although a few patients with more severe, refractory, or emergency clinical presentations will need specialist interventions, a large number of presentations can be effectively managed in primary care settings.

Evidence-based interventions for substance use disorders can be delivered through three broad platforms: population, community, and health-care platforms. Evidence for packages of care for substance use disorders is predominantly from high income countries and the evidence base is far less robust for LMICs. Best practice intervention packages based on evidence for their effectiveness in HIC or LMIC and contextual acceptability and scalability in LMICs are summarized here (Patel et al, 2016). Population level interventions for substance use disorders include regulating the availability and demand for alcohol (e.g. increased taxation) and penalization of risky behaviours associated with drinking (e.g. drunk driving). Community level interventions for alcohol include awareness campaigns to reduce maternal alcohol use during pregnancy. Primary care interventions include screening and brief interventions for alcohol use disorders and opioid substitution therapy for opioid dependence. Specialist care includes management of severe dependence and withdrawal, as well as psychological treatments such as CBT. The limited evidence available about cost effectiveness of interventions for substance use disorders indicate that brief interventions for harmful alcohol use fall towards the lower (more favourable) end of the spectrum for cost per DALY averted (Hyman et al, 2006; Chisholm & Saxena, 2012). Furthermore population based strategies such as increases in excise taxes, comprehensive advertising bans or reduced availability of retail outlets cost as little \$200–1200 per one DALY averted or \$0·10–0·30 per head in LMICs (Anderson, Chisholm & Fuhr, 2009).

Almost all evidence for packages of care for substance use disorders in LMICs is focused on alcohol use disorders. Recommendations for LMICs based on contextual evidence include opportunistic screening, stepped-care model, starting with brief advice and working up to extended brief interventions, community-based treatment of withdrawal (detoxification), structured relapse prevention in self-help groups, pharmacotherapy with disulfiram where family monitoring is available and with newer medications where available/affordable, follow up and monitoring in the community, and preventive interventions (Benegal, Chand & Obot, 2009). Furthermore, it is recommended that key tasks such as increasing consumer demand and awareness, increasing access and recognition, initiation of evidence based treatments, achievement of optimal recover/outcomes, and addressing the impacts of the disorder on other health and social outcomes, should all be addressed through primary care platforms (Benegal, Chand & Obot, 2009).

Barriers to access evidence based care

Despite existing evidence about the effectiveness of a range of packages of care for MNS disorders, a large proportion of persons across the world who are affected by such disorders do not have access to these interventions. The treatment gap for MNS disorders in LMICs is larger (>75%) as the resources are inadequate, inequitably distributed, and inefficiently used, and when available, care often is not evidence-based and of poor quality (Prince et al, 2007; Saraceno et al, 2007; Saxena et al, 2007). There are several reasons for the poor implementation of evidence based interventions in LMICs, the foremost being concerns about financial resources, and the low availability of appropriately trained specialist mental health workers. Furthermore, cultural attitudes, beliefs, and explanatory models about MNS disorders (e.g. MNS disorders seen as normative consequences of social adversity) lead to low demand for care and low visibility of the disorders from the perspective of health policy makers and providers (Aggarwal et al, 2014).Finally, stigma, poor awareness, and discrimination are other factors leading to low levels of political commitment to develop appropriate services and poor demand for care for people with MNS disorders (Saraceno et al, 2007).

The case for integrating services in primary care

In well-resourced settings persons with substance use disorders have access to medical clinicians, mental health clinicians, and substance abuse clinicians; each working in parallel systems and responding in a manner that reflects their respective training and background e.g. medical clinicians address the health consequences of using substances, mental health clinicians focus on the mental health issues secondary to substance use, and substance use clinicians focus on the individual's preoccupation with obtaining and consuming the substance. Thus, even if for the patient all these issues are equally critical he/she tends to fall into the cracks between these parallel and poorly inter-connected systems of care. On the other hand, in poorly resourced settings the only healthcare service available is primary care, which in many instances not equipped to deal with substance use disorders. However, in both these systems primary care remains the common factor and hence should be used more effectively as the care coordinating centre in a hub and spoke model in a high resourced setting or the frontline care delivery platform in low resourced settings.

Several cogent arguments have been made in favour of primary care providers taking a more proactive role in the management of substance use disorders (McLellan et al, 2000; Weaver, Jarvis & Schnoll, 1997). There are several advantages to such a model and these include access to comprehensive medical care for these vulnerable patients, improved preventive care, and improved linkages with addiction services reducing increased reliance on emergency services (Zechnich & Hedges, 1996; French and Martin, 1996; Himmelstein & Woolhandler, 1995; Stein et al, 2000).

On average, more than 70% of the adult population of most countries visit a doctor in a 12 month period and 70%-80% of those visit primary care physicians (Van Doorsaler et al, 2006), making primary care an excellent platform for frontline healthcare delivery. Beyond the clear advantage of greater coverage, it is well established that strong primary care health systems result in better and more equitable distribution of population health, and more effective use of resources (Kringos et al, 2010). These findings are not restricted to the developed world, and there is robust evidence that clearly demonstrates LMICs that make a political commitment to both education and primary care services achieve relatively high life expectancies despite low income (Cleland, 2010). Experiences from countries like Brazil,

Thailand, and Bolivia demonstrated that strengthening of primary care systems resulted in large reductions in infant and child mortality, chronic disease mortality, and hospitalizations for chronic diseases; and also overall decrease in healthcare inequities (Macinko et al, 2010; Macinko et al, 2011; Macinko et al, 2006; Vapattanawong et al, 2007; Perry et al, 1998; Reyes et al, 1998; Rosero - Bixby, 2004). Furthermore, evidence demonstrates that the success of primary care services in LMICs hinges on eliminating services directed at particular health problems and on providing integrated services, generally by non-physician primary care providers (Macinko et al, 2009; Kruk et al, 2010; Doherty & Govender, 2004).

However, despite the several opportunities afforded by primary care services in providing longitudinal, comprehensive, and coordinated care for substance use disorders, their potential has not been fully realized. There are several barriers to implementation of effective substance use disorder packages of care within primary care, even in developed countries. Some common barriers to implementation include insufficient time, lack of training in how to manage a positive screen, need to prioritise competing problems, stigmatization of substance abuse and scepticism about the effectiveness of counselling for substance use disorders (Van Hook et al, 2007; Rush et al, 1994; Beich, Gannik & Malterud, 2002; Aira et al, 2004; Johnson et al, 2010).

Innovating to strengthen primary care services in low resource settings

Clearly, in the absence of adequate specialist services, primary care services remain the most feasible and sustainable platform of care to effectively increase the access to care for people with substance use disorders.

One way of overcoming barrier to access is through task sharing in primary care i.e. rational redistribution of tasks among health workforce teams. Non-specialist health workers (NSHW) are one such human resource with which health care tasks can be shared. NSHWs are first-level providers who have received general rather than specialist mental health training and include professionals (doctors, nurses and other general paraprofessionals) as well as non-professionals (such as lay providers) (40). NSHWs trained and supervised by specialists have been able to effectively detect and treat mental disorders, refer appropriately, and provide psycho-education and follow-up care; and worked in a range of settings like clinics, halfway homes, and community outreach services, providing services for common mental disorders, severe mental disorders, epilepsy, learning disabilities, and dementia using complex stepped-care interventions, group interpersonal therapy, cognitive behavioural therapy, and psycho-educational programmes for caregivers (Van Ginneken et al, 2013; Araya et al, 2003; Bolton et al, 2003; Chatterjee et al, 2009; Dias et al, 2008; Patel et al, 2010; Rahman et al, 2008; Ran et al, 2003; Rojas et al, 2007; Xiang, Ran & Li, 1994). Compared to usual healthcare services, NSHWs have been shown to increase recovery from depression and/or anxiety, reduce symptoms in mothers with perinatal depression, reduce the symptoms of PTSD, improve the behavioural symptoms of people with dementia, improve mental well-being, burden and distress of carers of people with dementia, and decrease the amount of alcohol consumed by people with alcohol-use disorders (Van Ginneken et al, 2013). The evidence base for using NSHWs to deliver interventions for substance use disorders in LMICs is limited but encouraging. In a primary care based study from Thailand, Motivational Enhancement Therapy (MET) delivered by nurses to hazardous drinkers was significantly superior to 'assessment only' in reducing a range of risky drinking outcomes (Noknoy et al, 2010). In a HIV clinic based study from Kenya, Cognitive Behaviour Therapy (CBT) delivered by lay counsellors to hazardous or binge drinkers was superior to usual care and demonstrated large effect sizes (Papas et al, 2011).

Another innovative method to increase access to evidence based interventions for addictions is the use of technology as the delivery platform. Short messaging services (SMS) and Interactive Voice Response (IVR) [computer interacting with humans through the use of voice/keypad input] can be used to reach large numbers of people with addictions, quickly and at low cost. Furthermore, using IVR, barriers related to language and literacy can be overcome, and people in remote areas can be accessed with relative ease. There is extensive evidence to demonstrate that SMS/IVR can be used successfully to modify behaviours like smoking (Cole - Lewis & Kershaw, 2010). Although this innovation is relatively new to treatment of substance use disorders (Crombie et al, 2014; Aharonovich et al, 2016), it holds great potential for enhancing last mile healthcare delivery for these disorders. Internet based interventions represent another potentially effective option to prevention and treatment of substance use disorders, as they allow coverage of larger populations, at least in settings with good internet penetration, and can overcome some of the barriers to conventional face to face delivery of interventions. Interventions delivered through the internet arc inexpensive, overcome barriers related to geographical access, and availability and training of counsellors, and allow intervention delivery at the recipients' convenience. Evidence suggests that internet based interventions targeting alcohol-related problems have an effect about equivalent to brief face to face interventions (Tait & Christensen, 2010), and there is emerging evidence demonstrating the effectiveness of such interventions in preventing cannabis use (Walton et al, 2014).

However, in trying to increase access to interventions for substance use disorders, using traditional or innovative methods, it is important to remember that contextual differences play an important role in the development and treatment of substance use disorders as culture has a significant influence on differences in substance use histories, types of substances used, health consequences of substances used, attitudes towards substance use and treatment, pathways to treatment (and their interactions with issues like spirituality), and patterns of treatment engagement and retention (Strado & Donohue, 2006; Buser, 2009; Campbell et al, 2006; Iguchi et al, 2005; Jackson - Gilfort et al, 2001; Klonoff & Landrine, 2000; Moselhy & Telfer, 2002; Shillington & Clapp, 2003;). Hence along with developing psychosocial interventions that can be delivered by NSHWs, it is also important to develop interventions that are responsive to the context in which they will be delivered. An important factor that contributes to psychosocial interventions developed in western cultural contexts retaining their effectiveness in different cultural contexts, is the systematic methodology followed to make the adaptations (Chowdhary et al, 2014). In a recent primary care based study in India a contextually appropriate intervention developed using a systematic process and delivered by lay counsellors was effective in reducing drinking in male harmful drinkers (Nadkarni et al, 2017). The details of the intervention are described in Box 1.

Box 1: Counselling for Alcohol Problems (CAP)

The PRogrammE for Mental health Interventions in Under-resourced health systeMs (PREMIUM) a project in Goa, India aimed to develop psychosocial interventions for harmful drinking and depressive disorders based on both global and contextually relevant evidence and with emphasis on both acceptability to patients and feasibility for delivery by lay counsellors in routine health care settings. The intervention was developed using a framework that was informed by the Medical

Research Council (MRC) UK framework, previous intervention development experiences from the study setting, and a systematic review of contextual adaptations to psychosocial interventions. The intervention development process included understanding the available evidence and identifying gaps in the evidence for treatment of harmful drinking, proposing a theory about how the intervention might eventually work, assessing acceptability and feasibility of the intervention, and fine-tuning procedures for evaluation of the intervention.This process led to the development of Counselling for Alcohol Problems (CAP), a contextually appropriate psychosocial intervention package to be delivered by lay counsellors to harmful drinkers in primary care. The CAP intervention is designed to be delivered to harmful drinkers in three phases. In the 'initial phase' the counsellor helps the patient understand the problems his drinking may be causing and may need to change. This is done through a detailed assessment followed by personalised feedback. This is then used to facilitate a commitment to change from the patient which in turn is used to generate a 'change and action plan' which summarises what the patient wants to do to change his drinking and its related problems, and the actual actions that the patient will take to achieve this goal. In the 'middle phase' the counsellor helps the patient to develop 'thinking and behavioural' skills and techniques (drink refusal, handling drinking urges, problem solving and handling difficult emotions) that will allow the patient to make the changes that he desires. In the 'ending phase' the patient learns how to manage potential or actual relapses using these 'thinking and behavioural' skills and techniques. The common thread that runs across these phases is the counselling style of the counsellor, and that is informed by Motivational Interviewing (MI) and client centred supportive counselling. CAP is delivered over a maximum of four sessions, one session being considered a minimum requirement and two sessions being optimal. The sessions should ideally be delivered at a weekly to fortnightly frequency. Each session lasts 30 to 50 minutes and can span one or more 'phases' of CAP. For example, if a patient entering treatment is not ready for change then the complete first session would be focused on 'initial phase', but if a patient enters treatment ready for change then the counsellor could quickly move through the 'initial phase' in session 1 and proceed to the 'middle phase' in the same session. There is flexibility in where the intervention could be delivered based on the mutual convenience of the patient and the counsellor. The intervention could be delivered in the primary care clinic, patient's home, or in any other convenient but safe place (e.g. friend's home, village temple). Involving a significant other (SO) in the treatment is optional. It is recommended that the SO should be engaged as far as possible in the first session to get a better understanding of the patient's drinking and its impact, and also to help in developing a change plan. However, subsequent involvement of the SO may be encouraged based on how helpful the involvement was; and the patient and the counsellor should decide this collaboratively. Finally, the use of the information booklet is strongly recommended as it helps the patient engage with the treatment in between sessions. Thus the CAP has an inbuilt flexibility not just in what is delivered (i.e. the strategies used), but also in other aspects like where it is delivered (i.e. clinic, home, or any other alternative place), how it is delivered (i.e. phasic delivery), and who is involved in the treatment process (i.e. SO involved or not).CAP was tested in a large randomised controlled trial, where it was delivered to adult male harmful drinkers recruited from ten primary health centres in Goa, India. CAP was associated with strong effects on abstinence and remission at 3 months and these positive outcomes were sustained at 12 months. CAP is an example of contextually appropriate, effective, and potentially scalable intervention that can be delivered in primary care a relatively inexpensive and easily available human resource; thus increasing access to evidence based care for harmful drinking.

Conclusion

Substance use disorders contribute significantly to the burden directly attributed to mental, neurological and substance use disorders across the world. Despite the availability of evidence based models of care for substance use disorders there is a large treatment gap for these disorders. One way of reducing the treatment gap is to deliver the interventions through the primary care platform using innovations such as delivery using non specialist health workers and technology. There is growing evidence of the effectiveness of such models in the treatment of alcohol use disorders. Treatment of gambling disorders is at a nascent stage and translation and testing of successful models from the field of primary care management of alcohol use disorders to treat gambling disorders would be a good way forward.

Key points

- Mental health disorders and addictive disorders result in a large burden in terms of mortality, morbidity, or disability, and have high economic costs.
- In India, resources for treatment of addictive disorders including gambling are inadequate, inequitably distributed, and inefficiently used, and when available, care often is not evidence-based and of poor quality.
- In the absence of adequate specialist services, primary care services remain the most feasible and sustainable platform of care to effectively increase the access to care for people with addictive disorders.
- Although a minority will need specialist and inpatient treatment, a large number of those with gambling disorder can be effectively managed in primary care settings.
- Based on evidence from the alcohol use disorders field, the interventions that are best suited for delivery by non-specialists in primary care are brief interventions.

References

Aira, M., Kauhanen, J., Larivaara, P., Rautio, P. (2004). Differences in brief interventions on excessive drinking and smoking by primary care physicians: qualitative study. *Preventive Medicine*, 38(4):473-8.

Aggarwal, N. K., Balaji, M., Kumar, S., Mohanraj, R., Rahman, A., Verdeli, H. et al. (2014). Using consumer perspectives to inform the cultural adaptation of psychological treatments for depression: a mixed methods study from South Asia. *Journal of Affective Disorders*, 163:88-101.

Aharonovich, E., Hatzenbuehler, M., Johnston, B., O'leary, A., Morgenstern, J., Wainberg, M. et al. (2006). A low-cost, sustainable intervention for drinking reduction in the HIV primary care setting. *AIDS Care*, 18(6):561-8.

Anderson, P., Chisholm, D., Fuhr, D. C. (2009). Effectiveness and cost-effectiveness of policies and programmes to reduce the harm caused by alcohol. *The Lancet*, 373(9682):2234-46.

Araya, R., Rojas, G., Fritsch, R., Gaete, J., Rojas, M., Simon, G et al. (2003). Treating depression in primary care in low-income women in Santiago, Chile: a randomised controlled trial. *The Lancet*, 361(9362):995-1000.

Beich, A., Gannik, D., Malterud, K. (2002). Screening and brief intervention for excessive alcohol use: qualitative interview study of the experiences of general practitioners. *British Medical Journal*, 325(7369):870.

Benegal, V., Chand, P. K., Obot, I. S. (2009). Packages of Care for Alcohol Use Disorders in Low- And Middle-Income Countries. *PLoS Med*, 6(10):e1000170.

Bolton, P., Bass, J., Neugebauer, R., Verdeli, H., Clougherty, K. F., Wickramaratne, P. et al. (2003). Group interpersonal psychotherapy for depression in rural Uganda: a randomized controlled trial. *Journal of American Medical Association*,289(23):3117-24.

Buser, J. K. (2009).Treatment-seeking disparity between African Americans and Whites: Attitudes toward treatment, coping resources, and racism. *Journal of Multicultural Counseling and Development*, 37(2):94.

Campbell, C. I., Weisner, C., Sterling, S. (2006). Adolescents entering chemical dependency treatment in private managed care: ethnic differences in treatment initiation and retention. *Journal of Adolescent Health*, 38(4):343-50.

Carlbring, P. & Smit, F. (2008). Randomized trial of internet-delivered self-help with telephone support for pathological gamblers. *Journal of Consulting and Clinical Psychology* 76(6):1090.
Carlbring, P., Jonsson, J., Josephson, H., Forsberg, L. (2010). Motivational interviewing versus cognitive behavioral group therapy in the treatment of problem and pathological gambling: A randomized controlled trial. *Cognitive Behaviour Therapy.* 39(2):92-103.
Chatterjee, S., Pillai, A., Jain, S., Cohen, A., Patel, V. (2009). Outcomes of people with psychotic disorders in a community-based rehabilitation programme in rural India. *British Journal of Psychiatry.* 195(5):433-9.
Chisholm, D. & Saxena, S. (2012). Cost effectiveness of strategies to combat neuropsychiatric conditions in sub-Saharan Africa and South East Asia: mathematical modelling study. *British Medical Journal.* 344:e609.
Chowdhary, N., Jotheeswaran, A. T., Nadkarni, A., Hollon, S. D., King, M., Jordans, M. et al. (2014). The methods and outcomes of cultural adaptations of psychological treatments for depressive disorders: a systematic review. *Psychological medicine.* 44(6):1131-46.
Cleland, J. (2010). The benefits of educating women. *The Lancet.* 376(9745):933-4.
Cole-Lewis, H. & Kershaw, T. (2010). Text messaging as a tool for behavior change in disease prevention and management. *Epidemiologic reviews,* mxq004.
Crombie, I. K., Irvine, L., Williams, B., Sniehotta, F. F., Petrie, D., Evans, J. M. et al. (2014). A mobile phone intervention to reduce binge drinking among disadvantaged men: study protocol for a randomised controlled cost-effectiveness trial. *Trials,* 15(1):494.
Cunningham, J. A. (2005). Little use of treatment among problem gamblers. *Psychiatric Services,* 56(8):1024-a-5.
Degenhardt, L., Whiteford, H. A., Ferrari, A. J., Baxter, A. J., Charlson, F. J., Hall, W. D., et al. (2013). Global burden of disease attributable to illicit drug use and dependence: findings from the Global Burden of Disease Study 2010. *The Lancet.* 382(9904):1564-74.
Dias, A., Dewey, M. E., D'Souza, J., Dhume, R., Motghare, D. D., Shaji, K.S. et al. (2008). The effectiveness of a home care program for supporting caregivers of persons with dementia in developing countries: a randomised controlled trial from Goa, India. *PloS one.* 3(6):e2333.
Doherty, J & Govender, R. (2004). The cost-effectiveness of primary care services in developing countries: a review of the international literature. (file:///C:/Users/sanju.george/Downloads/The_Cost-Effectiveness_of_Primary_Care_Services_in%20(1).pdf)
Ezzati, M., Lopez, A. D., Rodgers, A., Vander Hoorn, S., Murray, C. J. L. (2002). Selected major risk factors and global and regional burden of disease. *The Lancet,* 360(9343):1347-60.
French, M.T. & Martin, R. F. (1996). The costs of drug abuse consequences: a summary of research findings. *Journal of Substance Abuse Treatment,* 13(6):453-66.
George, S, Gerada C. (2011). Problem gamblers in primary care: can GPs do more? : *British Journal of General Practice,* 61:754-56.
Gooding, P & Tarrier, N. (2009). A systematic review and meta-analysis of cognitive-behavioural interventions to reduce problem gambling: hedging our bets? *Behaviour Research and Therapy,* 47(7):592-607.
Himmelstein, D. U. & Woolhandler, S. (1995). Care denied: US residents who are unable to obtain needed medical services. *American Journal of Public Health,* 85(3):341-4.
Hodgins, D. C., Currie, S. R., el-Guebaly, N. (2001). Motivational enhancement and self-help treatments for problem gambling. *Journal of Consulting and Clinical Psychology* 69(1):50
Hodgins, D. C., Currie, S., el-Guebaly, N., Peden, N. (2004). Brief motivational treatment for problem gambling: a 24-month follow-up. *Psychology of Addictive Behaviors,* 18(3):293.
Hodgins, D. C., Toneatto, T., Makarchuk, K., Skinner, W., Vincent, S. (2007). Minimal treatment approaches for concerned significant others of problem gamblers: a randomized controlled trial. *Journal of Gambling Studies,* 23(2):215-30

Hodgins, D. C., Stea, J. N., Grant, J. E. (2007). Gambling disorders. *The Lancet*, 378(9806):1874-84.

Kaner, E. F., Beyer, F., Dickinson, H., Pienaar, E., Campbell, F., Schlesinger, C. et al. (2007). Effectiveness of brief alcohol interventions in primary care populations. *Cochrane Database* Syst Rev. 2007;2.

Hodgins, D.C., Currie, S.R., Currie, G., Fick, G. H. (2009). Randomized trial of brief motivational treatments for pathological gamblers: More is not necessarily better. *Journal of Consulting and Clinical Psychology;* 77(5):950.

Hyman, S., Chisholm, D., Kessler, R., Patel, V., Whiteford, H. (2006). Mental disorders. 1-20. In: Disease control priorities related to mental, neurological, developmental and substance abuse disorders. *Disease Control Priorities Project.* Eds: Jamison D. T., Breman J.G., Measham A.R., Alleyne, G., Claeson, M., David B Evans B. et al. Washington (DC): The International Bank for Reconstruction and Development / The World Bank; New York: Oxford University Press.

Iguchi, M. Y., Bell, J., Ramchand, R. N., Fain, T. (2005). How criminal system racial disparities may translate into health disparities. *Journal of Health Care for the Poor and Underserved.* 16(4):48-56.

Jackson-Gilfort, A., Liddle, H. A., Tejeda, M. J., Dakof, G. A. (2001). Facilitating engagement of African American male adolescents in family therapy: A cultural theme process study. *Journal of Black Psychology;* 27(3):321-40.

Johnson, E. E., Hamer, R., Nora, R. M., Tan, B., Eisenstein, N., Engelhart, C. (1997). The Lie/Bet Questionnaire for screening pathological gamblers. *Psychological Reports.* 80(1): 83-8.

Johnson, M., Jackson, R., Guillaume, L., Meier, P., Goyder, E. (2011). Barriers and facilitators to implementing screening and brief intervention for alcohol misuse: a systematic review of qualitative evidence. *Journal of Public Health,* 33(3):412-21

Klonoff, E. A. & Landrine, H. (2000). Revising and improving the African American acculturation scale. *Journal of Black Psychology;* 26(2):235-61.

Kringos, D. S., Boerma, W. G., Hutchinson, A., van der Zee, J., Groenewegen, P. P. (2010). The breadth of primary care: a systematic literature review of its core dimensions. *BMC Health Services Research,* 10(1):65.

Kruk, M. E., Porignon, D., Rockers, P. C., Van Lerberghe, W. (2010). The contribution of primary care to health and health systems in low-and middle-income countries: a critical review of major primary care initiatives. *Social Science & Medicine,* 70(6):904-11

Macinko, J., Guanais, F. C., De Souza, M. D. F. M. (2006). Evaluation of the impact of the Family Health Program on infant mortality in Brazil, 1990–2002. *Journal of Epidemiology and Community Health.* 60(1):13-9.

Macinko, J., Starfield, B., Erinosho, T. (2009). The Impact of Primary Healthcare on Population Health in Low and Middle Income Countries. *The Journal of Ambulatory Care Management.* 32(2):150-71.

Macinko, J., Dourado, I., Aquino, R., de Fátima Bonolo, P., Lima-Costa, M. F., Medina, M.G. et al. (2010). Major expansion of primary care in Brazil linked to decline in unnecessary hospitalization. *Health Affairs,* 29(12):2149-60.

Macinko, J., De Oliveira, V. B., Turci, M. A., Guanais, F. C., Bonolo, P. F., Lima-Costa, M. F. (2011). The influence of primary care and hospital supply on ambulatory care–sensitive hospitalizations among adults in Brazil, 1999–2007. *American Journal of Public Health.* 101(10):1963-70.

Makarchuk, K., Hodgins, D. C., Peden, N. (2002). Development of a brief intervention for concerned significant others of problem gamblers. *Addictive Disorders & Their Treatment*, 1(4):126-34.

McLellan, A. T., Lewis, D. C., O'brien, C. P., Kleber, H. D. (2000). Drug dependence, a chronic medical illness: implications for treatment, insurance, and outcomes evaluation. *Journal of American Medical Association*,284(13):1689-95.

Moselhy, H. F. & Telfer, I. (2002). The pattern of substance misuse among ethnic minorities in a community drug setting. *The European Journal of Psychiatry*, 16(4), 240-247.

Nadkarni, A., Weobong, B., Weiss, H. A., McCambridge, J., Bhat, B., Katti, B. et al. (2017). Counselling for Alcohol Problems (CAP), a lay counsellor-delivered brief psychological treatment for harmful drinking in men, in primary care in India: a randomised controlled trial. *The Lancet*, 389:186-95.

Noknoy, S., Rangsin, R., Saengcharnchai, P., McCambridge, J. (2010). RCT of effectiveness of motivational enhancement therapy delivered by nurses for hazardous drinkers in primary care units in Thailand. *Alcohol and Alcoholism*, 45(3):263-70

Pallesen, S., Mitsem, M., Kvale, G., Johnsen, B. H., Molde, H. (2005). Outcome of psychological treatments of pathological gambling: a review and meta analysis. *Addiction*, 100(10):1412-22.

Papas, R.K., Sidle, J. E., Gakinya, B. N., Baliddawa, J. B., Martino, S., Mwaniki, M.M. et al. (2011). Treatment outcomes of a stage 1 cognitive–behavioral trial to reduce alcohol use among human immunodeficiency virus-infected out-patients in western Kenya. *Addiction*, 106(12):2156-66.

Patel, V., Weiss, H. A., Chowdhary, N., Naik, S., Pednekar, S., Chatterjee S. et al. (2010). Effectiveness of an intervention led by lay health counsellors for depressive and anxiety disorders in primary care in Goa, India (MANAS): a cluster randomised controlled trial. *The Lancet*, 376(9758):2086-95.

Patel, V., Chisholm, D., Parikh, R., Charlson, F. J., Degenhardt, L., Dua, T. et al. (2016). Addressing the burden of mental, neurological, and substance use disorders: key messages from Disease Control Priorities, 3rd edition. *The Lancet*, 387(10028):1672-85.

Perry, H., Robison, N., Chavez, D., Taja, O., Hilari, C., Shanklin, D. et al. (1998). The census-based, impact-oriented approach: its effectiveness in promoting child health in Bolivia. *Health Policy and Planning*, 13(2):140-51.

Petry, N. M., Weinstock, J., Ledgerwood, D. M., Morasco, B. (2008). A randomized trial of brief interventions for problem and pathological gamblers. *Journal of Consulting and Clinical Psychology*, 76(2):318.

Prince, M., Patel, V., Saxena, S., Maj, M., Maselko, J., Phillips, M. R. et al. (2007). No health without mental health. *The Lancet*, 370(9590):859-77.

Rahman, A., Malik, A., Sikander, S., Roberts, C., Creed, F. (2008). Cognitive behaviour therapy-based intervention by community health workers for mothers with depression and their infants in rural Pakistan: a cluster-randomised controlled trial. *The Lancet*, 372(9642):902-9.

Ran, M-S., Xiang, M-Z., Chan, CL-W., Leff, J. (2003). Simpson P, Huang M-S, et al. Effectiveness of psychoeducational intervention for rural Chinese families experiencing schizophrenia. *Social Psychiatry and Psychiatric Epidemiology* 38(2):69-75.

Rehm, J., Mathers, C., Popova, S., Thavorncharoensap, M., Teerawattananon, Y., Patra, J. (2009). Global burden of disease and injury and economic cost attributable to alcohol use and alcohol-use disorders. *The Lancet*, 373(9682):2223-33.

Reyes, H., Pérez-Cuevas, R., Salmerón, J., Tomé, P., Guiscafré, H., Gutiérrez, G. (1998). Infant mortality due to acute respiratory infections: The influence of primary care processes. *Journal of Clinical Epidemiology,* 51:S12.

Rojas, G., Fritsch, R., Solis, J., Jadresic, E., Castillo, C., González, M. et al. (2007). Treatment of postnatal depression in low-income mothers in primary-care clinics in Santiago, Chile: a randomised controlled trial. *The Lancet,* 370(9599):1629-37.

Rosero-Bixby, L. (2004). Spatial access to health care in Costa Rica and its equity: a GIS-based study. *Social Science & Medicine,* 58(7):1271-84.

Rowan, M. S. & Galasso, C. S. (2000). Identifying office resource needs of Canadian physicians to help prevent, assess and treat patients with substance use and pathological gambling disorders. *Journal of Addictive Diseases,* 19(2):43-58.

Rush, B., Ellis, K., Crowe, T., Powell, L. (1994). How general practitioners view alcohol use. Clearing up the confusion. *Canadian Family Physician,* 40:1570.

Saraceno, B., van Ommeren, M., Batniji, R., Cohen, A., Gureje, O., Mahoney, J. et al. (2007). Barriers to improvement of mental health services in low-income and middle-income countries. *The Lancet.* 2007:370(9593):1164-74.

Saxena, S., Thornicroft, G., Knapp, M., Whiteford, H. (2007). Resources for mental health: scarcity, inequity, and inefficiency. *The Lancet,* 370(9590):878-89.

Shillington, A. M. & Clapp, J. D. (2003). Adolescents in public substance abuse treatment programs: The impacts of sex and race on referrals and outcomes. *Journal of Child & Adolescent Substance Abuse,* 12(4):69-91.

Slutske, W. S., Blaszczynski, A., Martin, N. G. (2009). Sex differences in the rates of recovery, treatment-seeking, and natural recovery in pathological gambling: results from an Australian community-based twin survey. *Twin Research and Human Genetics,* 12(05): 425-32.

Strada, M.J. & Donohue, B. (2006). Substance use in ethnic minority youth. *Journal of Ethnicity in Substance Abuse,* 5(1):67-89.

Stein, M. D., Urdaneta, M. E., Clarke, J., Maksad, J., Sobota, M., Hanna, L. et al. (2000). Use of antiretroviral therapies by HIV-infected persons receiving methadone maintenance. *Journal of Addictive Diseases,* 19(1):85-94.

Sullivan, S. (1999). Development of the" Eight" Problem Gambling Screen [thesis]. Auckland, New Zealand: Department of General Practice and Primary Care.

Tait, R. J. & Christensen, H. (2010). Internet-based interventions for young people with problematic substance use: a systematic review. *Medical Journal of Australia,* 192(11):S15.

Van Doorslaer, E., Masseria, C., Koolman, X. (2006). Group OHER. Inequalities in access to medical care by income in developed countries. *Canadian Medical Association Journal,* 174(2):177-83.

Van Ginneken, N., Tharyan, P., Lewin, S., Rao, G. N., Meera, S., Pian, J. et al. (2013). Non specialist health worker interventions for the care of mental, neurological and substance abuse disorders in low and middle income countries. *The Cochrane Library.*

Van Hook, S., Harris, S. K., Brooks, T., Carey, P., Kossack, R., Kulig, J. et al. (2007). The "Six T's": barriers to screening teens for substance abuse in primary care. *Journal of Adolescent Health,* 40(5):456-61.

Vapattanawong, P., Hogan, M. C., Hanvoravongchai, P., Gakidou, E., Vos, T., Lopez, A. D. et al. (2007). Reductions in child mortality levels and inequalities in Thailand: analysis of two censuses. *The Lancet,* 369(9564):850-5.

Walton, M. A., Resko, S., Barry, K. L., Chermack, S. T., Zucker, R. A., Zimmerman, M. A. et al. (2014). A randomized controlled trial testing the efficacy of a brief cannabis universal prevention program among adolescents in primary care. *Addiction,* 109(5):786-97.
Weaver, M. F., Jarvis, M. A., Schnoll, S. H. (1999). Role of the primary care physician in problems of substance abuse. *Archives of Internal Medicine,* 159(9):913-24.
Whiteford, H. A., Degenhardt, L., Rehm, J., Baxter, A. J, Ferrari, A. J., Erskine, H. E. et al. (2013). Global burden of disease attributable to mental and substance use disorders: findings from the Global Burden of Disease Study 2010. *The Lancet,* 382(9904):1575-86.
World Health Organization. (2008). Scaling up care for mental, neurological, and substance use disorders.
World Health Organization . (2008). The global burden of disease: 2004 update. 2008.
Xiang, M., Ran, M., Li, S. (1994). A controlled evaluation of psychoeducational family intervention in a rural Chinese community. *British Journal of Psychiatry,* 165(4):544-8.
Zechnich, A. D. & Hedges, J. R. (1996). Community–wide emergency department visits by patients suspected of drug–seeking behavior. *Academic Emergency Medicine,* 3(4):312-7.

Chapter 11

Finding a place for gambling addiction in Indian psychiatry

Roy Kallivayalil and Arun Enara

Introduction

Gambling addiction does not occupy a place within mainstream Indian psychiatry or addiction psychiatry. This is the case in terms of research, strategy and treatment provision. Although multiple stakeholders such as psychiatrists, policy makers, the Government, gambling industry, etc. are all, to varying degrees, responsible for this state of affairs, in this chapter we will focus on what psychiatrists in India and Indian psychiatry in general can do to change the status quo.

Up until the Diagnostic and Statistical Manual of Mental Disorders V (DSM V) (APA, 2013) included "gambling disorder" in the section on addictive disorders, it was shrouded in nosological ambiguity. Gambling disorder now sits alongside other substance addictions (the criterion which relates to "committing illegal acts to gamble such as forgery, fraud, theft or embezzlement" has been deleted as this on its own is rarely endorsed when other criteria are not fulfilled). The deletion of this criterion would mean that in DSM V, a diagnosis of disordered gambling can be made if four of the nine (as opposed to 5 out of 10 in DSM IV) criteria are met. This move will help confer gambling addiction with the status of a valid psychiatric disorder and as an addictive disorder.

Why should this change?

Gambling addiction negatively impacts on the gambler, his/her family and the wider society.

Gambling addicts have high rates of physical and psychiatric comorbidity.

They tend to report higher rates of various psychosomatic symptoms (cardiovascular, musculoskeletal, gastrointestinal and other non - specific psychosomatic symptoms) (Morasco et al, 2006), and psychiatric problems such as depression, anxiety, substance misuse and personality disorders. (Petry et al, 2005)

Although gambling addiction has not been extensively studied in India, two studies estimated the prevalence of gambling and problem gambling among school (Jaisoorya et al, 2017) and college students (George et al, 2016) in India and found the following: only a quarter of school and college students in India reported having ever gambled (this is much lower than that found in other studies of young people in other parts of the world); and 7.1% of the sample were identified as problem gamblers. Perhaps most importantly, of those students who ever gambled, a quarter (25.2%)\ were classified as problem gamblers suggesting that in India there are significantly high rates of problem gambling among those who gamble. They also found that problem gamblers when compared with non-gamblers were significantly more likely to have poor academic performance, higher lifetime use of alcohol, tobacco and cannabis, greater psychological distress, more suicidal thoughts and attempts, and higher ADHD symptom scores . So, from the data available it is clear that gambling is a problem in India.

Views of Indian psychiatrists

In 2014, George et al surveyed 121 Indian psychiatrists who attended the 2012 Annual National Conference of Indian Psychiatric Society in Kochi, Kerala. The survey sample, albeit a convenience sample, was representative in terms of age, gender, place of work, setting of psychiatric practice and years of experience in psychiatry. 79% (96/121) of those surveyed said that they see gamblers in their clinical practice, and 62% (75/121) said they also see those affected by someone else's gambling habit. However, 89 of the 121 (74%) psychiatrists admitted that they had never received any teaching in the management of gambling addiction. More encouragingly, the large majority of those surveyed (109/121) saw treatment of gambling addiction as being within their remit, and most (105/121) also considered it feasible to treat gambling addicts within their mainstream psychiatric practice. 77% (93/121) said that they would like to receive more training.

Perhaps, the most important finding was that while most psychiatrists see gamblers and their loved ones, very few psychiatrists are well equipped to treat them. It was particularly encouraging to note that most psychiatrists were eager to receive more training in this regard and considered it feasible to treat gamblers in their mainstream general psychiatric practice.

It follows from the above that there are significant gaps in the training of psychiatrists, if they are to be adequately equipped to treat gambling addicts and their affected families. Given the willingness expressed by psychiatrists, it will be a shame not to seize this opportunity and act.

What can psychiatrists do?

It is clear that Indian psychiatrists come across gambling addicts and affected families in their day-to-day clinical practice but the large majority of these psychiatrists have had no training/teaching in this field. However more encouragingly, most psychiatrists we surveyed expressed a desire to improve matters and they saw identification and treatment of gambling addiction as being within their remit, and perceived this to be feasible. Hence plugging this gap should be a priority.

Once psychiatrists are adequately and appropriately trained, they can screen those patients who are deemed at high risk, such as those presenting with psychosomatic symptoms, other psychiatric disorders including substance misuse, depression, and anxiety-spectrum disorders, and those reporting financial problems. And all those who screen positive for gambling problems ought to be signposted or treated in the appropriate setting.

In India, sensitivity to problem/pathological gambling is quite low. Discourses on gambling disorder often take a moral model to explain the difficulties experienced by this group. Very few think of gambling disorder as a medical/mental health problem. Gambling in India is either viewed as a vice or suppressed by the legal and executive arms of the government, or as a popular taxable commodity, often taken advantage of by the finance department of the government. These models often promote the development of underground syndicates and also cause harm to the vulnerable. Psychiatrists have a wider responsibility here to conceptualize and present gambling as a public health issue that warrants more attention. As to why gambling is an important public health problem in India is discussed in depth in a previous chapter of this book.

In addition to the obvious education and training of psychiatrists, and provision of treatment, at a more strategic level there is a desperate need for further research in this field in India. It is here, that in addition to psychiatrists, mental health policy makers and academics too have key roles and responsibilities in conceiving and driving a coherent gambling harm prevention strategy, which looks comprehensively into its research, education and treatment.

Indian psychiatry can no longer avoid this issue. The call is for more education, treatment and research into gambling addiction in India. Indian psychiatrists have a crucial role to drive this agenda forward, drawing on international evidence and collaborations and helping to formulate policies and laws consistent with current knowledge and evidence.

Conclusion

Having looked at why psychiatrists should do more and what they could do, there is reason to be optimistic. The Indian Psychiatric Society (IPS) has taken some steps in the right direction in this regard: IPS in 2015 published a booklet on behavioural addictions and gambling addiction features significantly in it. (file:///C:/Users/sanju.george/Downloads/OTHER%20PUTATIVE%20BEHAVIOURAL%20ADDICTIONS.pdf). Let us hope that, going forward, gambling addiction features more prominently in Indian psychiatry.

Key points

- Gambling addiction does not occupy a place within mainstream Indian psychiatry.
- Psychiatrists, at the very least, should screen those patients who are deemed at high risk, such as those presenting with psychosomatic symptoms, other psychiatric disorders including substance misuse, depression, and anxiety-spectrum disorders for gambling problems.
- Those who screen positive for gambling problems ought to be signposted or treated in the appropriate setting.
- There is need for more education, treatment and research into gambling addiction in India. Indian psychiatrists have a crucial role to drive this agenda forward, drawing on international evidence and collaborations, and helping to formulate policies and laws consistent with current knowledge and evidence.

References

American Psychiatric Association. Diagnostic and Statistical Manual of Mental Disorders (5th edn) (DSM-5). APA, 2013.

George, S., Jaisoorya, T.S., Sivasankaran, N.B., Rani, A., Menon, P., Madhavan, R. et al. (2016). A cross-sectional study of problem gambling and its correlates among college students in South India. *British Journal of Psychiatry Open, 2 (3)*:199- 203.

George, S., Kallivayalil, R., Jaisoorya, T. S. (2014). Gambling addiction in India: Should psychiatrists care? *Indian Journal of Psychiatry.* 56 (2): 111-112.

Jaisoorya, T. S., Beena, K. V., Beena, M., Ellangovan, K., Thennarassu, K., Bowden-Jones H. et al. (2017). Do High School Students in India Gamble? A Study of Problem Gambling

and Its Correlates. *Journal of Gambling Studies*. 33(2):449-460
Morasco, B. J., Pietrzak, R. H., Blanco, C., Grant, B. F., Hasin, D., Petry, N. M. et al. (2006). Health problems and medical utilization associated with gambling disorders: results from the National Epidemiologic Survey on Alcohol and Related Conditions. *Psychosomatic Medicine*, 68: 976 – 84
Petry, N.M., Stinson, F. S., Grant, B. F. (2005). Comorbidity of DSM –IV pathological gambling and other psychiatric disorders: results from the National Epidemiologic Survey on Alcohol and Related Conditions. *Journal of Clinical Psychiatry*, 66: 564–74.

Chapter 12

Gambling in India: The future

Sanju George and Jaisoorya TS

Gambling and gambling-related harm are likely to increase over the coming years in India. This is because of lack of awareness among the general public about gambling's potential risk for addiction, weak anti-gambling legislation, a societal move to ape the West, existing plans in some states to open casinos as a means to generate tax revenue for the government, and the growing popularity of online gambling opportunities with more Indians accessing the internet on their phones, laptops and so on.

Here we are not attempting to predict what the future of gambling will be like in India but merely try to foresee some key challenges that this area will face and will offer some thoughts on how best to face them. We have listed some of them below:

1. Gambling legislation needs to be modernised. The law that regulates gambling in India is the Public Gambling Act of 1867 (The Public Gambling Act, 1867 [Internet]). It was enacted by the Imperial Legislative Council with a view to regulate and discourage gambling on games of chance. It restricted most forms of gambling and also discriminated between what it saw as games of pure chance such as Satta (which it made illegal) from games of skill and not just mere chance such as horse racing (which it made legal). Currently the Centre has devolved exclusive powers to individual states to deem what types of gambling are legal or illegal.

It is reasonable to say that this piece of legislation is archaic and needs revision, primarily because the gambling landscape in India has changed a lot since 1867. The law could be made more fit for purpose so it can address some of the 'gaps' given below: punishments for breaking the law are very mild and not detracting enough - punishment for being found in a gaming house is a fine of Rupees 100; it excludes 'games of mere skill' - betting on horse racing being deemed a game of skill; the Act's remit does not include online gambling; as the Centre has devolved powers to individual states, there is considerable variation in how individual states and Union Territories interpret this Act; there needs to tighter legislation to address the issue of online gambling; etc.

There also needs to be a wider debate to address how strict should gambling legislation be in India: Should it be completely illegal or should it be fully legalized? Other intermediate options include banning specific types of gambling while permitting others, banning or legalising certain gambling venues such as casinos, opening more betting shops that are tightly regulated and taxed, etc. We suggest maintaining status quo for now, while more research (especially population-based public health research) is undertaken to help formulate evidence-based policies.

2. Need to take a public health approach to gambling and gambling-related harm: Problem gambling is an important public health issue because of its prevalence, increased risk to certain vulnerable groups, and its numerous physical, psychological and social adverse consequences to the gambler, his/her family and the wider society (Roaf, 2015).

Hence there also needs to be a public health approach aimed at reducing gambling-related harm and associated problems. As this is discussed in depth in the chapter on gambling and public health, we will limit our discussion here: A three-level approach for the prevention of gambling-related problems, consisting of primary, secondary and tertiary levels of prevention ought to be considered (George et al, 2017). Primary prevention measures aim to prevent gambling from becoming a problem; they target all gamblers and non-gamblers. They focus on social, psychological and legal strategies. Examples of primary prevention strategies include awareness-raising campaigns about various aspects of gambling, its potential for harm, signs and symptoms, how to seek help, banning and enforcing thereof (in both print and online media) of gambling advertisements and promotions, and the increasing in-counter-advertising, etc. Secondary prevention measures aim at early diagnosis and treatment, and they target at-risk and problem gamblers. Examples of secondary prevention measures include providing training to staff at gambling venues (casinos and lottery shops) to enable them to recognise problem gamblers; training non-specialists (primary health care staff, mental health care staff, etc.) in early identification of individuals who experience gambling-related harm, and training them in providing brief psychological interventions for problem gamblers, etc. Tertiary prevention strategies target individuals experiencing harm from their own gambling or through their loved one's gambling.It includes specialist and intense psychological and psychiatric interventions for problem gamblers and support for their families.

3. More research needs to be done: Perhaps this is stating the obvious but its importance of this cannot and should not be under estimated. As has been clear from the chapter on 'Gambling research from India', very little has been done to date. We still know very little about gambling in India. Or in other words, there is no evidence base to inform policy making or treatment. There is no data on the prevalence of gambling and gambling-related problems in India, or its prevalence in specific populations, its correlates and comorbidity, course and outcome, treatment effectiveness, etc.

It is crucial to have answers to the above research questions because the first question any policy maker will ask of any well-intentioned researcher or academic who tries/hopes to convince the policy maker of gambling's risk will be- 'But, where is the evidence?'. Similarly, if one wishes to work with the gambling industry wanting them to adopt socially responsible gambling policies, the industry will ask - 'Maybe gambling can cause harm but where is the research from India to back this claim?'

4. What can Indian psychiatry and its psychiatrists do?

First and foremost, psychiatrists need to give gambling addiction its rightful place within mainstream psychiatry, very much like substance addictions. It will then follow that any academic discourse that is had re addictions will automatically include gambling as well. And for any such academic discourse to produce meaningful outcomes, it is best for it to be under the auspices of the Indian Psychiatric Society (IPS) - initiated and led by IPS but involving all relevant parties such as academics, health care professionals, NGOs working in this field, gambling industry, policy makers, etc. Psychiatrists should be key stakeholders in this debate, and they could start by giving gambling addiction a place within mainstream psychiatry. Indian psychiatry, through the Indian Psychiatric Society, has taken some positive steps in the above direction, and the publication 'Clinical practice guidelines on Newer and Emerging Addictive Disorders in India' is an example (2016). However, IPS hasn't issued a position statement on gambling addiction.

Second, psychiatrists themselves are less than adequately aware of gambling addiction, its signs and symptoms, screening, assessment and treatment (George et al, 2014). There is a desperate need to offer training packages addressing areas noted above, to psychiatrists and other allied healthcare professionals.

Third, psychiatrists should also be aware of secondary and tertiary public health level measures to prevent gambling-related harm. These include screening, offering brief psychological interventions, and appropriately specialized psychological and pharmacological interventions for gamblers and their families. Not all psychiatrists need to offer all treatment interventions themselves but at least ought to be aware of these, and where feasible offer what they can, and where not feasible signpost patients and families to the appropriate agency.

Finally, psychiatrists also need to lead on carrying out more research in the field of gambling, problem gambling and gambling-related harm. A starting point could be a community-based prevalence study of gambling participation and problem gambling.

5. Who will fund gambling treatment services?

Here, once could either take the view that 'polluter' pays, and thereby require the gambling industry to fund treatment services. Or as is the case for treatment of substance addiction (alcohol and drugs), the government could fund at least some treatment services. To be ethically sound, provision of gambling treatment should be independent of the gambling industry (Walker and George, 2013). 'Independent' treatment providers could include the government or charitable organisations. This might be easier said than done, given the prevailing economic climate in mental health treatment funding. It might be more pragmatic to try a combined funding stream involving both the government and the gambling industry. A strict ethical code of practice for the industry's involvement would need to be imposed and monitored, to allay any ethical concerns.

6. Gambling treatment service provision: An integrated four – tier addictions model

Gambling treatment services can be offered at four tiers/levels, depending on whether the treatment is offered by a specialist or not and whether what is offered is generic or very specific/specialized (George and Copello, 2011): ***They include:***

Tier 1 - non-specialist/generic services that provide information, screening and onward referral.

Tier 2 - specialist services that offer interventions such as advice, harm reduction and brief psychological interventions.

Tier 3 - specialists offering care-planned and structured treatments such as cognitive behaviour therapy, group therapy and pharmacotherapies.

Tier 4 - Residential treatment programs.

Given the resource limitations within Indian addictions services, it makes more sense to integrate gambling treatment services within the existing network of drug and alcohol treatment services. This would be the most cost-efficient and sustainable way to deliver services and to enhance existing service provision. Major advantages of using existing drug and alcohol treatment services as a vehicle to deliver gambling treatment are the infrastructure and personnel cost efficiencies in terms of not generating separate set-up and running costs. There will be some additional investment requirements primarily in terms of staff training and support to ensure their skill set broadens enough to include gambling treatment interventions. There might also be a need to increase personnel capacity, dependent on the volume of additional activity this generates. All this can only successfully happen if existing addiction treatment services are fully signed up to this, both strategically and operationally.

7. A gambling strategy and a body to oversee it

Developing a national gambling strategy and having an independent body to oversee it are key to minimising gambling-related harm. Such an independent body ought to include experts from the fields of gambling research, treatment, policy and academia. It could advise the government on the research, education and treatment aspects of gambling; and determine what research, education and treatment is required to reduce harm from gambling. It should also cover all forms of gambling and set the agenda for gambling operators, regulators, commissioning organisations, government, trade bodies, treatment providers and several other public agencies.

Lastly and perhaps most importantly, to bring all the above strands of work into a coherent whole, there needs to exist a body/organisation that could lead on, direct and co-ordinate, and in turn advice the government on all aspects of research into, and education and treatment of gambling. It goes without saying that all interested parties need to take part in any such discussion, although participation of the gambling industry should come with some caveats to prevent self-interests.

References

Basu, D., Dalal P.K., Balhara, Y.P.S. (Eds). (2016). Clinical Practice Guidelines on Newer and Emerging Addictive Disorders in India'. Indian Psychiatric Society.

George, S. & Copello, A. (2011). Treatment provision for Britain's problem gamblers: present gaps and future opportunities. *Advances in Psychiatric Treatment*, 17 (5) 318-322

George, S., Velleman, R., Nadkarni, A. (2017). Gambling in India: Past, present and future. *Asian Journal of Psychiatry*: 26: 39 – 43.

George, S., Kallivayalil, R., Jaisoorya, T.S. (2014). Gambling addiction in India: Should psychiatrists care? *Indian Journal of Psychiatry*, 56 (2): 111 – 112.

Roaf, E. (2015).Gambling and public health. In: Bowden-Jones, H, & George, S. (Eds.), A Clinician's Guide to Working with Problem Gamblers. Routledge, London.

The Public Gambling Act, 1867 [Internet]) Sangrur Police; [cited 2017 May 5]. Available from: http://www.sangrurpolice.in/wpcontent/themes/intrepidity/images/actrule/publicGamblingAct1867.pdf)

Walker, T. & George S. (2013). Funding treatment for gambling addiction in Great Britain: ethical issues. *British Journal of Hospital Medicine*, 74(5): 246 – 47.